DEDICATION

This book is dedicated to John, my best friend and dedicated husband of fifty-five wonderful years. He has eaten many leftovers, helped with household duties and sacrificed his time so I could write. Thank you for being my strong support, believing in me and encouraging me to do what God placed in my heart. I will love you forever!

AM I REALLY A CHRISTIAN?
Exploring Salvation and Beyond

TRIBUTE
PUBLISHING
2018

Copyright © 2018
Tribute Publishing LLC
Frisco, Texas

Tribute Publishing, LLC

Am I Really a Christian?
First Edition January 2018

All Worldwide Rights Reserved
ISBN: 978-0-9998358-1-4

All Rights Reserved. No part of this book may be reproduced, stored in a retrieval system, or transmitted, in any form, or by any means, electronic, mechanical, recorded, photocopied, or otherwise, without the prior written permission of the copyright owner or the Author, except by a reviewer who may quote brief passages in a review.

Printed in the United States of America.

In God We Trust.

FOREWORD

Have you ever been asked, "If you died today and went to the gates of heaven, and the gatekeeper asked you, 'Why should I allow you to enter heaven?' what would your reason for admittance be?" This question has been asked many times of hundreds, if not thousands, of people with about as many varying answers. Few people seem to understand God's requirements for eternal life with Him. All people *will* live forever! The question is, "Where?"

Maybe you know the answer, maybe not. Perhaps you call yourself a Christian, but doubts at times cloud your mind and you long to know *for sure* that your eternal destiny is heaven. This book takes you on a journey to find out what it means to be a Christian and to have the peace and assurance that you long for. Searching questions will be asked and Biblical answers supplied to those who may have doubts about their eternal destiny or simply want to explore and clarify what being a Christian involves. Some of the topics discussed include: What is Christianity? What are some of the erroneous beliefs? What is sin? Who is Satan? Who is Jesus? What is salvation? What is baptism? What is a covenant relationship? Who is the Holy Spirit? How do good works and fruit fit in? How can one become a Christian? and What will help one live a Christian life? Many sub-topics are covered to help bring understanding and encouragement to those seeking truth.

Of necessity, many Scriptures have been presented within the text with others referenced for you to research. In no way are any of the subjects discussed in this book intended to be a complete theological discussion. We have merely scratched the surface of truth to be found in God's Word. You are encouraged to research for yourself, gain understanding through group Bible studies, and seek fellowship in a Bible-centered church and among dedicated Christian friends. Although this has not been written in a typical study format, I believe it would lend itself well to either personal or group study.

Our hope is for you to find clarity to answers you may have, to discover how much God loves you, and to settle once and for all your eternal destiny.

Unless otherwise indicated, all Scriptures have been taken from the New International Version (NIV). Many words and/or phrases have been italicized, bolded or underlined for emphasis, which are solely those of this author.

CONTENTS

Introduction i

Chapter 1 – What It Means to Be a Christian 1

Chapter 2 – The Question of Sin 7

Chapter 3 – One Is Your Friend; the Other Isn't 15

Chapter 4 – Exploring Salvation 27

Chapter 5 – A Covenant Relationship 47

Chapter 6 – Ready for the Adventure 61

Chapter 7 – Being Sure of My Destiny 73

Chapter 8 – New Behaviors, New Attitudes 81

Chapter 9 – Becoming a Disciple or Follower 93

Chapter 10 – Change Points 105

Chapter 11 – Encountering Adversity 123

Chapter 12 – God's Provisions – Our Heritage 131

Chapter 13 – GPS - to Keep Us on Track 145

Chapter 14 – Wrapping It Up 161

Helpful Resources 169

About the Author, Dorothy Smith 173

INTRODUCTION

What Does It Take?

I had never left the country before and felt a little uneasy as I approached the security gate. This was the ultimate vacation, a sort of reward after a lifetime of hard work. I had been thinking a lot lately about this particular trip, with a bit of apprehension, for sure, but also with the expectancy of a young child who had been promised a reward. I had heard that each traveler was carefully screened and that certain requirements must be met. Reliable sources had assured me, however, that I would most certainly be qualified.

I strained my neck, peering past others in line, so I could see up ahead. The attendant at the gate seemed kindly enough, as he conversed with other travelers. He even looked strangely familiar to me. But then, I had met many people in my lifetime. As I began to focus on fellow travelers closest to the gate, my apprehension grew. Several people had been turned away and were now frantically searching through their belongings for something – I did not know what. Now I wondered if indeed I had all the proper credentials. I was in the middle of a mental checklist when my name was called.

"Do you have your authorization?" the attendant asked. I pulled out a xeroxed copy of my church membership and my almost flawless attendance record. Most of my absences were "excused," I was sure, but there were a few questionable ones.

"Sir, how many unexcused absences do you allow?" I asked timidly.

"That's not what I need," he replied.

I then produced letters of recommendation from people who knew me and could attest to my faithfulness in prayer and service. He simply shook his head. Confidently, I handed him my impressive list of deeds through the years that chronicled each time I gave or helped or smiled or prayed. Now the list seemed much shorter than I remembered, and my mind was suddenly asking, *how many deeds were enough to qualify me?* He merely glanced at the list and handed it back.

I was becoming a little annoyed now. I had spent years producing these documents – serving on committees, teaching Sunday School, singing in the choir, playing the piano, leading youth groups, helping with Vacation Bible School. Why, I had held prestigious positions, not only in church, but in charitable organizations as well. I had been a child advocate, served the underprivileged, collected food and clothing for the needy. I had a rather impressive resume, if I did say so myself.

I reached into my life portfolio to see what else I had brought. Oh yes, the set of tapes on which were recorded all the theological debates in which I had engaged over the years. Here was concrete *proof* of my knowledge of the Bible. Surely that would give me an edge over these other less qualified individuals. I looked up at the attendant expecting to see his smile of approval. Instead, he was looking at me with incredible sadness in his eyes.

"What is it you need to see?" I demanded, now thoroughly irritated.
"Your faith," he replied quietly.

"My faith," I stuttered. "What does faith have to do with anything? What about all these? Don't they count for anything?"

Without answering me, he pulled out two books. The title of the first book was *Qualified for Heaven* and the other read, *Destined for the Lake of Fire*. I waited expectantly as he opened the first volume and searched under the alphabetic listing for my name. Time seemed to be suspended like there was no yesterday and no tomorrow. As he closed the first book and reached for the second volume, I felt myself becoming sick with fear. "Did you look under my maiden name?" I cried out. "Maybe you overlooked it; my name has to be there." A violent, uncontrollable shudder went through me, like the aftershock of an earthquake as the realization of my situation washed over me. All of life seemed to capsulize into this one moment. I was consumed with grief, and the self-righteous evidence I had brought with me suddenly evaporated into insignificance.

"No!" I cried. "No, it can't be. I'm a good person. I always went to church. I did all these things." And I shook the handful of papers and tapes in his face.

"Yes," he replied. "We know all these things about you. But God's requirements for heaven are clearly stated in the instruction book for mankind, the Bible. Nowhere does it state that good works or church membership or self-righteousness is a ticket to heaven. No mortal can ever earn or deserve the privilege of eternal life with a totally holy, just, righteous God through his own efforts. God made provision for each man, woman, and child, through his son, Jesus Christ, but man wants to do it his own way."

"Please," I cried. "Won't you reconsider?"

Hebrews 2:3 says, "How shall we escape if we ignore such a great salvation?" Indeed, it is a great salvation, an incredible gift. Why do we think we have a better plan and ignore God's plan for allowing us to live eternally with him? Why do we wait, when none of us has a clue how long, or short, our life may be? Proverbs 14:12 reminds us, "There is a way that seems right to a man, but in the end it leads to death."

In John 6:37-40, Jesus tells us that "whoever comes to me I will never drive away. For I have come down from heaven not to do my will, but to do the will of him who sent me. And this is the will of him who sent me, that I shall lose none of all those he has given me, but raise them up at the last day. For *my Father's will is that everyone who looks to the Son and believes in him shall have eternal life*, and I will raise them up at the last day."

> *Are you looking for eternal life in all the wrong places?*

What It Means to Be a Christian

What It Means to Be a Christian

CHAPTER 1

What It Means to Be a Christian

What *does* it mean to be a Christian? Ask almost anyone on the streets in America and, unless they are an avowed atheist, the majority will tell you they are a Christian. Or at least they think they might be. Many have been reared in homes where church attendance or reading the Bible or even talking about spiritual matters was seldom done. And yet they call themselves Christians or somehow think they might qualify. So what does qualify us? This we will explore. Can we *know* without a doubt that we are a Christian, or must we simply *hope* we are one? The answer is a resounding, "Yes, we can know." We don't have to wonder. We don't have to wait until we die and then have a "surprise party."

To many people, Christian is merely a title. During a lifetime we can have a number of titles. We usually start out as the child of so-and-so, then the spouse of someone, after the little ones arrive we become the parent of such-and-such child, and on down the line until we may finally achieve our own identity. Most titles are the result of some type of relationship, either family, business, educational, or social. The title of 'Christian' also identifies a relationship, the most vital relationship any man or woman will ever have. In fact, our eternal destiny hinges on this relationship. As we explore what it means to be a Christian, it is our hope that you can lay aside all preconceived ideas and look carefully at what the Bible really says. In its pages we can find honest answers to honest questions.

Through the centuries, a number of false concepts contrary to the teachings of the Bible have developed regarding salvation and what it means to be a Christian. Many people both inside and outside the walls of the church have a false sense of security (or insecurity) as to where they will spend eternity simply because they do not understand what salvation is according to the Word of God. Others believe they cannot know their eternal destiny, but can only *hope* they make it to heaven when they die. Some have invented their own doctrines and declare "they have their own thing going" with God. And, sad to say, many misconceptions have originated in the pulpits of our churches; some are born out of ignorance as to what the Bible teaches, others are simply what we have chosen to believe.

Erroneous concepts concerning salvation will most certainly beg the question of who can rightfully call themselves a Christian. Some believe that being a Christian means living in a "Christian" nation, being a good person, or doing benevolent things. Others are convinced it's putting one's name on a church membership roll, affiliation with a particular denomination, or being reared in a Christian home. Some even believe that reading the Bible, praying now and then, going to church, or naming the Name of Jesus qualifies them as a Christian. These may help get one on the right path and be the means of bringing one *to* salvation, but trusting in any one of these *for* salvation is a deadly deception. Neither is it sufficient to know *about* God, to know intellectually who Jesus is, or even understand the plan of salvation. It's what we *do* about what we know that counts. It's *acting* on what we understand and *living* in its truth. It's the choice we make to accept or reject the gift that God offers which determines our eternal destiny. Thus, in order to understand what salvation is or even why it is necessary, we must answer some important questions.

Who is a Christian?

A Christian is one who has accepted God's love and His provision for salvation through His Son, Jesus Christ. He is totally committed to serving God; Christ is both Savior and Lord of his life. He has received a new heart that desires God's will above his own and he has made a commitment to live in covenant relationship with God. Because of his life-changing encounter with the living Lord, he has made the decision to no longer live for "self" but for God. He is willing to lay aside all self-seeking, self-love, idolatry, lust, and unholy activity and walk in humble obedience and repentance toward God. He is allowing the Holy Spirit to grow him, mature him and change him into the image of Jesus. There is evidence of "good fruit" being produced in his life. This one is a Christian. So we must ask ourselves . . .

Am I really a Christian?

Before you start thinking, "There's *no way* I could ever be a Christian according to those standards," let me assure you that God has provided not only the means, but also the ability. You take the first step toward God, and he will provide everything you need to live an abundant Christian life.

I remember following a guide through the maze of a cave far below the surface of the earth. The path was well-lighted, and we could see the deep caverns and dangerous crevices along the way. We could hear the gurgling of an underground stream far below us. After crawling along a narrow, slippery ledge, we arrived in a large room resembling a small amphitheater. The guide instructed us to sit down and then he turned off all the lights. I have never experienced such blackness. What would happen if any one of us tried to find our way out of that cave with no light and no guide? It was a frightening thought. Just as the guide in that cave would lead us along the right path and safely out, so will God on our journey. He doesn't leave us to stumble around groping in the darkness. He becomes our light *and* our guide.

"Your word is a lamp to my feet and a light for my path" (Psalm 119:105).

In this study, we will attempt to dispel misconceptions and provide as accurate a picture as possible. This is certainly not an exhaustive study, but one which we hope will help you *know* if your eternal destiny is secure.

What is Christianity?

Simply put, Christianity has its beginning, its fulfillment, and its end in Almighty God, Creator of the universe, and in Jesus Christ, God's Son, who carried out God's eternal plan of redemption for all mankind through the power and work of the Holy Spirit. Christianity is the *only* religion in which God is the pursuer, a God of love who actively seeks out man, initiates fellowship, and provides the means for reconciliation.

Ephesians 1:4
> "For he (God) chose us in him before the creation of the world."

Luke 19:10
> "For the Son of Man came to seek and to save what was lost."

In all other religions, God is depicted as a distant, unapproachable being, who seems to have little, if any, cordial feelings toward humankind. He doesn't appear to even *like* us, much less *love* us. Man is the pursuer, who tries to appease this unreachable god through various religious exercises and good works; thus, man becomes the means of his own salvation through self-effort. Other religions base their teachings on the ideas, philosophies, or ethics of the men who founded their religion. Christianity is based on the events of creation, the plan of redemption, and the person of Jesus Christ, who he is and what he did.

What It Means to Be a Christian

John 3:16-17
> "For God so loved the world that he gave his one and only Son, that whoever believes in him shall not perish but have eternal life. For God did not send his Son into the world to condemn the world, but to save the world through him."

Historical and scientific evidence for the Christian faith is overwhelming. Many excellent books are available which explore these evidences and proofs. Probably the most compelling evidence is the personal witness of the Holy Spirit in the lives of hundreds of thousands of individuals down through the ages. The intention of this study is not to argue the authenticity of the Christian faith, but to simply present Biblical truth concerning salvation and what it means to be a Christian. Each subject discussed will be verified by Scripture, with additional verses indicated below each topic. I strongly encourage you to do your own research. Some helpful tools would be a Bible in an easy-to-understand translation, (New International Version, The Message Bible, the Voice) a complete concordance, a Bible dictionary, and a topical index. A number of resources are listed in the Notes section at the back of the book.

The following chapters will explore some of the basic elements of the Christian faith and attempt to answer questions that might typically be asked by those who seek to understand and know the truth. It is our deepest hope that your search for truth will lead you to the *only* One who can say,

> *"I am the way and the truth and the life."*
> *John 14:6*

What It Means to Be a Christian

Chapter 2

The Question of Sin

<u>What is Sin?</u>

This sounds like a simple question, yet it probes into right and wrong, good and evil, truth and falsehood, obedience or rebellion as set forth by God himself. The Creator, who made us and put into us something of himself, is the only one who has the *right* and the *power* to know and tell us what is good and bad for us. And God did just that. He set forth absolutes and standards by which to live. He established the law and instructed man to obey it.

Exodus 21:1
> The Lord said to Moses, "These are the laws you are to set before them."

Leviticus 25:18
> On Mount Sinai the Lord told Moses to tell the people, "Follow my decrees and be careful to obey my laws."

Romans 7:7
> "I would not have known what sin was except through the law."

If there is no law, there is no violation. If we had no speed limits posted on our streets and highways, we could drive any speed we wanted and there would be no violation. Without law it would be perfectly alright for every person to do what is right in their own eyes. You could set the standard and the rules for yourself. And without God, that is exactly what man does, for he does not recognize the authority and sovereignty of the one and only God, Creator of heaven and earth. Man makes himself the authority, deciding what is right and wrong based on what he thinks will make him happy. And that is the very basis of sin – SELF. Self is the "I will do as I please" attitude that sets itself against the laws of God. This was the sin found in Lucifer (Satan) that led to his rebellion and fall, which will be covered in more detail later. And this is the attitude that is in our world today.

Likewise, *if there is no standard, there is no absolute*. What would happen if we had no standard units of measure? Suppose Carpenter A made himself a measuring stick with 13 inches as a foot. Carpenter B decided he liked a smaller unit, so he made himself a ruler with 11 inches as a foot. Can you imagine the chaos when they tried to build a house together – especially if the one who laid the foundation had used 12 inches as a foot? The standard unit of measure is an absolute for all the world. So it is with God's standards; they become the absolutes for all mankind from which we anchor our system of values. Sadly, man down through the ages has rebelled against God's absolutes so he can engage in any kind of behavior he chooses. Then he tries to convince the world that his behavior is acceptable and there should be laws to protect him. As a society begins to tolerate more and more perverseness and move farther and farther from God's absolutes, we careen toward inevitable destruction. In the final scheme of things, however, man *will* account to God – and we *will* be judged according to God's standards. God's laws have not changed.

Romans 14:10b, 12

> "For we will all stand before God's judgment seat. So then, each of us will give an account of himself to God."

God gave the first <u>law</u> in Genesis 2:16-17. "And the Lord God commanded the man, 'You are free to eat from any tree in the garden; but *you must not eat from the tree of the knowledge of good and evil,* for when you eat of it you will surely die.'"

Man's first transgression is recorded in Genesis 3 when Eve listened to the serpent, the great deceiver Satan, and made a *choice* to disobey God and eat of the forbidden fruit. Adam *chose* to take the fruit Eve offered him and eat what God had told them not to eat. At that moment, Adam and Eve entered into lawlessness – they broke God's law, they disobeyed, they did not believe what God said was true, they did what they believed was right in their own eyes. They did what they thought would make them happy. The devil lied to them and they CHOSE to believe his lies. Read Genesis 3:1-7 and notice Satan's deception and lies as well as Adam and Eve's decisive choice. The Bible defines sin as the following:

Lawlessness

1 John 3:4
> "Everyone who sins breaks the law; in fact, *sin is lawlessness.*"

Disobedience

Rom. 5:19
> "For just as through the *disobedience* of the one man (Adam) the many were *made sinners,* so also through the obedience of the one man (Jesus Christ) the many will be made righteous."

Walking in Rebellion to God

Ps. 78:56
> "But they put God to the test and *rebelled* against the Most High; they did not keep his statutes."

Heb. 3:15-18

> "... today if you hear his voice, do not harden your hearts as you did in the *rebellion*. Who were they who heard and *rebelled?* Were they not all those Moses led out of Egypt? And with whom was he (God) angry for forty years? Was it not with those who sinned, whose bodies fell in the desert? And to whom did God swear that they would never enter his rest if not to those who disobeyed?"

Choosing to Believe the Lies of the Devil

II Thess. 2:9, 10

> "The coming of the lawless one will be in accordance with the work of Satan displayed in all kinds of counterfeit miracles, signs and wonders, and in every sort of evil that *deceives* those who are perishing. They perish because *they refuse to love the truth* and so be saved."

Wrongdoing

I John 5:17

> "All wrongdoing is sin ..."

Faithlessness (unbelief)

Rom. 14:23

> "... everything that does not come from faith is in." NOTE: *Faith is believing and accepting that what God said is true.*

Revelation 21:8

> "But the cowardly, *the unbelieving*, the vile, the murderers, the sexually immoral, those who practice magic arts, the idolaters and all liars – their place will be in the fiery lake of burning sulfur."

(See also 2 Thess. 2:12; Romans 11:20; and Hebrews 3:12)

> *Are you excusing things in your life that God calls sin?*

Must every person deal with the *sin* problem?

The answer is YES! We were all born into this world without the slightest possibility of being able to live a sinless life. Did you have to teach your child to be self-centered and demanding, to tell lies, to be possessive, selfish and destructive? Indeed not. Parents spend most of their time correcting *wrong* behavior and teaching little ones what is *right*. Thanks to Adam and Eve, we were all born with a sin nature, and everyone must deal with the sin problem. Adam and Eve introduced sin into the world and along with sin comes death and condemnation. Jesus introduced righteousness into the world and along with it eternal life and forgiveness.

Ecclesiastes 7:20
> "There is *not a righteous man on earth* who does what is right and never sins."

Romans 3:23
> "For *all have sinned* and fall short of the glory of God..."

(See also Romans 3:9-12; Romans 5:12; Psalm 51:5; Psalm 58:3)

The Question of Sin

What happens if we don't deal with the *sin* problem?

Sin separates us from God, and we remain in that condition unless we deal with the sin problem. Separation from God means eternal death. God created man not only to care for the earth and rule over the animals, He established communication and fellowship with him. How awesome is that? But that was the plan; God wanted fellowship with those whom He had created in His image. When Adam and Eve committed the first sin, alienation from God was the consequence, and they were driven out of the garden and out of the presence of God. All mankind is born with a sin nature, which must be recognized and dealt with, or he will remain eternally alienated from God.

Romans 5:12

> "Therefore, just as sin entered the world through one man, and death through sin, and in this way *death came to all men*, because all sinned."

Then why did God allow sin to enter the world?

Because God made us creatures of choice, not pre-programmed robots, he will not violate our right to choose. With the first command came an option to obey or not obey; Adam and Eve made a choice. We, too, must make a choice. Unless we make the *choice* to leave the kingdom of darkness (Satan's) and enter the kingdom of light (God's), we will remain forever under the control of Satan. That means that if you have never made the choice to accept God's gift of eternal life through Jesus, when you die, you will not go to heaven. You will spend eternity in hell separated from God. Every person must make the decision *before* he dies where he will spend eternity *after* he dies.

Isaiah 59:2

> "But your iniquities have separated you from your God; your sins have hidden his face from you, so that he will not hear."

Romans 6:23
> "For the wages of sin is death . . ."

There are only two kingdoms – the kingdom of God and the kingdom of darkness. There is no fence to sit on. There is no neutral zone. We are either a member of one kingdom or a member of the other. We cannot be a citizen of both kingdoms. We cannot serve two masters.

James 4:4
> "You adulterous people, don't you know that friendship with the world is hatred toward God? Anyone who chooses to be a friend of the world becomes an enemy of God."

Matthew 6:24
> "No one is able to serve two masters; for either he will hate the one and love the other, or he will stand by and be devoted to the one and despise the other. You cannot serve God and mammon - riches, that is, or anything in which you trust and on which you rely." (The Amplified Bible)

Notice in the first verse from James, he calls them an "adulterous people." An adulterer is one who has not remained faithful to the one he/she has vowed to love. Perhaps we say we love God, but want to maintain unhealthy, ungodly ties to sinful behavior. This is how verses 4 and 5 in the Message Bible reads:

> "You're cheating on God. If all you want is your own way, flirting with the world every chance you get, you end up enemies of God and his way. And do you suppose God doesn't care? The proverb has it that 'he's a fiercely jealous lover.' And what he gives in love is far better than anything else you'll find."

Before we go further, let's take a look at both the one who controls the kingdom of darkness (and ultimately our destiny if we choose to live and remain apart from God), and the one who made it possible to live forever with our Heavenly Father.

> *To which kingdom do you belong?*

Chapter 3

One Is Your Friend; the Other Isn't

You may be the most well-loved person on the planet, but you do have one enemy. His name is Satan and he is real. Although most of us call him the devil, several names are used in Scripture to identify him:

> Abaddon (Rev. 9:11), accuser (Rev. 12:10), adversary (1 Peter 5:8), angel of the abyss and Apollyon (Rev. 9:11), Belial (2 Cor. 6:15), Beelzebub (Matt. 12:24), devil (Matt. 4:1 and James 4:7), dragon (Rev. 12:7; 13:2; 20:2), evil one (Matt. 13:19), god or prince of this world (2 Cor. 4:4 and John 14:30), Lucifer (Isa. 14:12), murderer, liar and father of lies (John 8:44), prince of the power of the air (Eph. 2:2), ruler of darkness (Eph. 6:12), ruler of the demons (Matt. 12:24), serpent (Gen. 3:4), tempter (Matt. 4:3).

Satan was an angelic created being, once perfect, who rebelled against God and was expelled from heaven. Jesus himself witnessed Satan's expulsion and told his disciples: "I saw Satan fall like lightning from heaven" (Luke 10:18). Satan's goal was to usurp God's throne and authority, and he continues to fight for the right to rule men's lives. It is believed that demons are fallen angels who joined him in his rebellion and may have constituted as many as one third of the angels.

Revelation 12:3-4
> "Then another sign appeared in heaven: an enormous red dragon. His tail swept a third of the stars out of the sky and flung them to the earth."

Revelation 12:7-9

> "And there was war in heaven. Michael and his angels fought against the dragon, and the dragon and his angels fought back. But he was not strong enough, and they lost their place in heaven. The great dragon was hurled down--that ancient serpent called the devil, or Satan, who leads the whole world astray. He was hurtled to the earth, and his angels with him."

We are given a glimpse of what will happen to Satan and his final outcome in the last book of the Bible.

Revelation 20:10

> "And the devil . . . was thrown into the lake of burning sulfur, where the beast and the false prophet had been thrown. They will be tormented day and night for ever and ever."

Interesting pictures are given in Isaiah and Ezekiel that scholars believe refer to Satan (Lucifer), even though the prophecies may also refer to former earthly kings of Tyre and Babylon.

Isaiah 14:12-15

> "How you have fallen from heaven, O morning star, son of the dawn! You have been cast down to the earth, you who once laid low the nations! You said in your heart, 'I will ascend to heaven; I will raise my throne above the stars of God; I will sit enthroned on the mount of assembly, on the utmost heights of the sacred mountain. I will ascend above the tops of the clouds; I will make myself like the Most High.' But you are brought down to the grave, to the depths of the pit."

One Is Your Friend; the Other Isn't

Ezekiel 28:12-17

> "You were the model of perfection, full of wisdom and perfect in beauty. You were in Eden, the garden of God; every precious stone adorned you: ruby, topaz and emerald, chrysolite, onyx and jasper, sapphire, turquoise and beryl. Your settings and mountings were made of gold; on the day you were created they were prepared. You were anointed as a guardian cherub, for so I ordained you. You were on the holy mount of God; you walked among the fiery stones. You were blameless in your ways from the day you were created till wickedness was found in you. Through your widespread trade you were filled with violence, and you sinned. So I drove you in disgrace from the mount of God, and I expelled you, O guardian cherub, from among the fiery stones. Your heart became proud on account of your beauty, and you corrupted your wisdom because of your splendor. So I threw you to the earth; I made a spectacle of you before kings."

Satan is very real and so are his demons; the Bible speaks plainly of his existence, power, influence, and final outcome. Even though Satan is the "prince (or god) of this world," man does not have to remain under his control. God Almighty, Maker of heaven and earth, brought about a plan of redemption through his Son Jesus Christ to give man a choice.

1 John 3:8

> "The reason the Son of God appeared was to destroy the devil's work."

John 14:30

> And just before his death, Jesus told his disciples that "the prince of this world is coming. He has no hold on me."

The person who has received Jesus Christ as his Savior and is actively living in obedience to God has been transferred out of Satan's kingdom and into God's kingdom. Satan no longer has any legal right to rule his life. Although the devil has no legal right to someone, he will try to harass and discourage and tempt people to sin. Peter tells us, "Your enemy the devil prowls around like a roaring lion looking for someone to devour. Resist him, standing firm in the faith" (1 Peter 5:8, 9a). The good news is, we have been given power, authority and weapons to stand against all the evil schemes and tactics of the devil.

Colossians 1:13-14
> "For he (God) has rescued us from the dominion of darkness and brought us into the kingdom of the Son he loves, in whom we have redemption, the forgiveness of sins."

Luke 10:19
> Jesus said, "I have given you authority to trample on snakes and scorpions and to overcome all the power of the enemy; nothing will harm you."

Ephesians 6:10-12
> "Finally, be strong in the Lord and in his mighty power. Put on the full armor of God so that you can take your stand against the devil's schemes. For our struggle is not against flesh and blood, but against the rulers, against the authorities, against the powers of this dark world and against the spiritual forces of evil in the heavenly realms."

(See also 2 Cor. 10:4; 1 Peter 5:8,9; James 4:7, 8; & Eph. 6:13-17)

> *Are you standing against the devil's attacks, or are you allowing him to wreak havoc in your life?*

Who is Jesus?

More good news is that you have a *best* friend, and his name is Jesus. Other names used throughout the Bible to identify him are:

> Christ (Mark 8:29), Lord (Matt. 4:7), Savior (2 Peter 2:20), Son of Man (Matt. 8:20), Son of God (1 John 5:13), Messiah (John 1:41), Lamb of God (John 1:29), Prince of Peace (Isaiah 9:6), Immanuel (Matt. 1:23), the Alpha and Omega (Rev. 1:8), Mediator (1 Timothy 2:5), Holy One (Mark 1:24), High Priest (Hebrews 2:17), King of the Jews (Matt. 27:11), Lion of Judah (Rev. 5:5), Light of the World (John 8:12), Root & Offspring of David and Bright Morning Star (Rev. 22:16), Redeemer (Isaiah 48:17), Good Shepherd (John 10:11, 14), Bread of Life (John 6:35), the Way, the Truth, the Life (John 14:6), True Vine (John 15:1, 5), Rock (Psalm 19:14), Chief Cornerstone (Eph. 2:20), Master (Matt. 23:8), Anointed One (Daniel 9:26 & Acts 10:38), the Almighty (Rev. 4:8), King of Kings and Lord of Lords (Rev. 17:14).

Jesus is like no one who has ever lived on this planet. It is fascinating to consider the vast number of Old Testament prophecies that were fulfilled in the New Testament, many of which contained specific references to the Messiah that were fulfilled in Jesus. These prophecies were not vague, but contained detailed and specific information. The fact that these prophecies came through *numerous* prophets over several hundred years and were all written *at least* 250 to 800 years before Jesus' birth makes it even more phenomenal. Only an all-knowing God could accomplish such a thing. To help you do further research, several books are listed in the Notes section in the back. The following are some of the important truths we need to know about Jesus.

<u>He is the divine Son of God</u>. The angel, who appeared to the virgin Mary, gave him the name Jesus, which means Savior (Luke 1:26-33); at his baptism, God himself spoke from heaven to confirm his deity (Luke 3:21-22); angels announced his birth to shepherds (Luke 2:8-20); Simeon and Anna knew who he was when he was presented at the temple (see Luke 2:25-38); even demons recognized him (see Luke 8:26-39).

Matthew 3:17
> "And suddenly a voice came from heaven saying, 'This is My beloved Son, in whom I am well pleased.'"

Luke 22:70
> "Then they all said, 'Are you then the Son of God?' So He said to them, 'You rightly say that I am.'"

Matthew 16:16
> "Simon Peter answered and said, 'You are the Christ, the Son of the living God.'"

<u>He was with God in the beginning</u>.

John 1:1-2
> "In the beginning was the Word (Jesus) and the Word was with God and the Word was God. He was in the beginning with God.

John 8:58
> "'I tell you the truth,' Jesus answered, 'before Abraham was born, I am!'"

John 17:5
> "And now, Father, glorify me in your presence with the glory I had with you before the world began."

<u>He is creator of all things</u>.

Colossians 1:16
> "For by Him (Jesus) all things were created; things in heaven and on earth, visible and invisible, whether thrones or powers or rulers or authorities; all things were created by him and for him."

John 1:3
> "All things were made through Him, and without Him nothing was made that was made."

<u>He became man</u>. Although he was fully God, he became fully man to identify with our humanity.

Galatians 4:4-5
> "But when the time had fully come, God sent his Son, born of a woman, born under law, to redeem those under law, that we might receive the full rights of sons."

Philippians 2:8
> "And being found in appearance as a man, he humbled himself and became obedient to death – even death on a cross."

<u>He lived a sinless life.</u>

2 Cor. 5:21
> "God made him *who had no sin* to be sin for us, so that in him we might become the righteousness of God."

1 Peter 2:22
> "He *committed no sin*, and no deceit was found in his mouth."

Hebrews 4:15
> "For we do not have a high priest who is unable to sympathize with our weaknesses, but we have one who has been tempted in every way, just as we are — *yet was without sin.*"

1 John 3:5
> "But you know that he appeared so that he might take away our sins. *And in him is no sin.*"

<u>His death on the cross (shedding His blood) paid for our sins.</u>

1 Cor. 15:3
> "For what I received I passed on to you as of first importance: that Christ died for our sins."

Matthew 26:28
> "This is my blood of the covenant, which is poured out for many for the forgiveness of sins."

1 John 1:7
> ". . . and the blood of Jesus, his Son, purifies us from all sin."

<u>He is the only way, the only mediator between God and man</u>. Some religions teach that all paths lead to God, but that is not what the Bible teaches.

1 Timothy 2:5-6
> "For there is one God and one mediator between God and men, the man Christ Jesus, who gave himself as a ransom for all men."

John 14:6
> Jesus answered, "I am the way and the truth and the life. No one comes to the Father except through me."

<u>His bodily resurrection is the crowning point and absolute proof of Christianity</u>. No other religious leader, earthly king or ruler, however great or holy, has ever been resurrected. They each died, their bodies were buried, and they all remained in their graves. Jesus knew he would die and be resurrected, and he openly made this known to others.

John 2:19-22
> "Jesus answered and said to them, 'Destroy this temple, and in three days I will raise it up.' Then the Jews said, 'It has taken forty-six years to build this temple, and will You raise it up in three days?' But He was speaking of the temple of His body. Therefore, when He had risen from the dead, His disciples remembered that He had said this to them; and they believed the Scripture and the word which Jesus had said."

Acts 13:36, 37
> "For when David had served God's purpose in his own generation, he fell asleep; he was buried with his fathers and his body decayed. But the one

whom God raised from the dead did not see decay."

The resurrection was not just hearsay. Jesus appeared to the eleven disciples on several occasions, to other individuals, to a crowd of more than 500 people, and later to Paul. There were eye witnesses that Jesus was actually alive; he walked, talked, ate and drank with them. He even showed them his scars from the beatings and crucifixion and invited them to touch him to know he was real.

Acts 2:32

> "This Jesus God has raised up, of which we are all witnesses."

Luke 24:36-43

> "While they were still talking about this, Jesus himself stood among them and said to them, 'Peace be with you.' They were startled and frightened, thinking they saw a ghost. He said to them, 'Why are you troubled, and why do doubts rise in your minds? Look at my hands and my feet. It is I myself! Touch me and see; a ghost does not have flesh and bones, as you see I have.' When he had said this, he showed them his hands and feet. And while they still did not believe it because of joy and amazement, he asked them, 'Do you have anything here to eat?' They gave him a piece of broiled fish, and he took it and ate it in their presence."

Acts 1:3

> "After his suffering, he showed himself to these men and gave many convincing proofs that he was alive. He appeared to them over a period of forty days and spoke about the kingdom of God."

One Is Your Friend; the Other Isn't

(Also read Luke 24:13-35 and John, chapters 20 and 21.)

<u>Jesus is fully God.</u> He is not merely a prophet or a great teacher, an angel or a created being, as some religions teach. He is a member of the Godhead, the second person of the Trinity. Thus, God was able to reveal who He is in the person of Jesus.

Hebrews 1:3
> "The Son is the radiance of God's glory and the exact representation of his being, sustaining all things by his powerful word."

John 10:30
> "I and the Father are one."

(See also Romans 9:5)

> *Do you believe Jesus is who the Bible says he is?*

Accepting the truth of who Jesus is becomes the catalyst to understanding the gift of salvation. God offers to each of us, a plan to pay the penalty for sins for which we deserve to die.

One Is Your Friend; the Other Isn't

Chapter 4

Exploring Salvation

<u>What is Salvation?</u>

Salvation is both an *event* and a *process*. The first step is a life-changing encounter with the living God. It is a decision to become a follower of Jesus. Some call it being "saved," "born again," "redeemed," or "becoming a child of God." It matters little what words we choose to describe our initiation into the Kingdom of God. The importance lies in our continuing relationship with Jesus Christ, which is the process. From here on, we will be making daily decisions to either live for self or live for God, to resist the Holy Spirit or allow Him to work in and through us. In two simple words, salvation is being "in Christ."

<u>Salvation is God's way of paying for our SIN</u>

So why does sin have to be paid for? God would not be just if He simply excused our sin – it must be dealt with fitly and correctly. Let's suppose a person guilty of committing a serious crime stood before a certain judge. There is no doubt of his guilt, and the crime deserves the death penalty. To everyone's amazement, the judge simply shakes his head and says, "Oh, he didn't mean to do those things; he was just having a bad day. Anyway, I know the man and that's just the way he is – he's only human, you know." So he excuses the man and calls for the next case, which he handles in the same manner. Has justice been served? Would you consider him a just judge? Of course not! Justice calls for accountability; justice demands reward or penalty, as the matter deserves.

God is totally just. We have *all* sinned; we *all* deserve punishment. God cannot and will not simply excuse our sins. Instead, He actually arranged for someone else to take the punishment we deserve. This He accomplished through his Son, Jesus Christ, who actually took our place and paid for our sins so we wouldn't have to. But it is still our choice: we can pay the penalty for our own sins, which is eternal death (see Romans 6:23), or we can accept the gift payment which Jesus Christ made. There are no other terms – there are no other options.

Acts 4:12

> "Salvation is found in no one else, for there is no other name under heaven given to men by which we must be saved." (Verse 10 identifies Jesus Christ and his name.)

Acts 10:43

> "All the prophets testify about him (Jesus) that everyone who believes in him receives forgiveness of sins through his name."

(See also John 10:9; Romans 5:8; and Matthew 1:21)

<u>It is God's gift to mankind</u>. No one can buy it, earn it or deserve it. Salvation is the greatest, most outrageous gift ever.

Rom. 6:23

> "For the wages of sin is death, but *the gift of God* is eternal life in Christ Jesus our Lord."

Eph. 2:8, 9

> "For it is by grace you have been saved, through faith – and this not from yourselves, *it is the gift of God* – not by works, so that no one can boast."

It is a _covenant_ with Almighty God to love Him with all our heart, soul, mind, and strength and to carefully obey Him. These particular commands are found over and over in God's original covenant with Israel found in Deuteronomy and in the new covenant with all believers. The meaning of covenant is discussed in more detail later.

Deuteronomy 6:3a, 5
> "Hear, O Israel, and be careful to obey so that it may go well with you ... Love the Lord your God with all your heart and with all your soul and with all your strength."

Matthew 22:37-38
> "Jesus replied, 'Love the Lord your God with all your heart and with all your soul and with all your mind. This is the first and greatest commandment.'"

It is the beginning of a new way of life. Becoming a Christian is like having an "extreme makeover" on the inside. And you can be assured it will show on the outside.

2 Corinthians 5:17
> "Therefore, if anyone is in Christ, he is _a new creation_; the old has gone, the new has come!"

Romans 6:4
> "We were therefore buried with him through baptism into death in order that, just as Christ was raised from the dead through the glory of the Father, _we too may live a new life._"

It is a starting point for spiritual fellowship with Christ, with God the Father, and with other believers in which we no longer walk in darkness but walk in light. The fellowship which was broken when Adam sinned is restored.

1 John 1:3

> "We proclaim to you what we have seen and heard, so that you also may have fellowship with us. And our fellowship is with the Father and with his Son, Jesus Christ."

1 John 1:5-7

> "This is the message we have heard from him and declare to you: God is light; in him there is no darkness at all. If we claim to have fellowship with him yet walk in the darkness, we lie and do not live by the truth. But if we walk in the light, as he is in the light, we have fellowship with one another, and the blood of Jesus, his Son, purifies us from all sin."

<u>It is the beginning of a process</u>, a life-long journey committed to serving and following Jesus Christ.

Luke 14:27

> "Anyone who does not carry his cross and *follow me* cannot be my disciple."

John 10:27

> "My sheep *listen* to my voice; I know them, and they *follow* me."

John 12:26

> "Whoever serves me must *follow me*; and where I am, my servant also will be."

The reason we hesitate to be a *follower*, is because we don't fully trust the one *leading*. We are afraid of where he might be taking us. I remember watching the cattle in the distance as my husband walked ahead of them, calling them to follow him. We would often shut the cattle out of certain areas to allow the grass to grow, then move them to the "greener pasture" when it was time.

A few of the older cows who knew John's voice followed him willingly; some even jumped and frolicked ahead of him as if delighted to be with him. The majority of cows, however, continued to graze, looking up now and then, but content to stay where they were. I thought, "If those silly cows only knew where they were being led and the succulent grass that awaited them, they would be eager to follow." We are much like those cattle – content with where we are, hesitant to leave the familiar for the unknown. Little do we realize the great and abundant things God has in store for us, if only we would follow. When we get to really *know* our Shepherd, we understand that he *always* has our best interests in mind; he is always working for our good.

Romans 8:28
>"And we know that in all things God works for the good of those who love him, who have been called according to his purpose."

> *Do you recognize the voice of your Shepherd?*
> *Are you joyfully following?*

What Does Salvation Do? When one says, "Yes, I want to be a follower of Jesus. I believe he died to pay for my sins," a transaction has taken place which has immediate results.

Reconciles us to God. Reconciliation is making peace between enemies.

Romans 5:10
> ". . . when we were God's enemies, we were *reconciled* to him through the death of his Son . . ."

2 Cor. 5:18-19
> "All this is from God, who *reconciled us to himself* through Christ and gave us the ministry of reconciliation: that God was *reconciling the world to himself* in Christ, not counting men's sins against them."

(See also Romans 5:11; and Colossians 1:20)

<u>Justifies us</u>. A just God declares us to be "not guilty."

Romans 3:23-24
> "For all have sinned and fall short of the glory of God, and all are *justified freely by his grace* through the redemption that came by Christ Jesus."

Romans 4:25
> "He (Jesus) was delivered over to death for our sins and was *raised to life for our justification*."

(See also 1 Corinthians 6:11; Isaiah 53:11; Romans 5:1, 9, 16, 18; Romans 8:30)

<u>Gives us the right to become God's children and his heirs</u>.

John 1:12
> "Yet to all who received him, to those who believed in his name, he *gave the right* to become children of God" (dependent on our believing and receiving).

Romans 8:16, 17

> "The Spirit himself testifies with our spirit that we are *God's children*. Now *if we are children, then we are heirs* -- heirs of God and co-heirs with Christ, if indeed we share in his sufferings in order that we may also share in his glory" (dependent on sharing his sufferings).

(See also Romans 8:13-15)

Transfers us from Satan's kingdom (darkness) to God's kingdom (light).

Col. 1:13, 14

> "For he has rescued us from the *dominion of darkness* and brought us into the *kingdom of the Son* he loves, in whom we have redemption, the forgiveness of sins."

Acts 26:17b-18

> Paul relates the message he received from Jesus on the road to Damascus at his conversion: "I am sending you to them to open their eyes and turn them from *darkness to light, and from the power of Satan to God*, so that they may receive forgiveness of sins and a place among those who are sanctified by faith in me."

Clothes us with Christ's righteousness and holiness.

II Cor. 5:21

> "God made him who had no sin to be sin for us, so that in him we might *become the righteousness of God*."

I Cor. 1:30
> "It is because of him that you are in Christ Jesus, who has become for us wisdom from God -- that is, *our righteousness, holiness, and redemption.*"

(See also Philippians 3:9)

<u>Gives us eternal life.</u>

John 3:16
> "For God so loved the world that he gave his one and only Son, that whoever believes in him shall not perish but *have eternal life.*"

John 3:36
> "*Whoever believes in the Son has eternal life*, but whoever rejects the Son will not see life, for God's wrath remains on him."

(See also John 5:29; 5:40; 11:25, 26; and 1 John 5:11, 12)

I have heard people make the statement, "We are all God's children." Actually, no we're not - not in the sense that we're speaking of in this discussion. Yes, God created each of us and made us in his image, giving us intelligence above all other creatures. He equipped each of us, not only with a body, but also a soul and spirit capable of responding to him and entering into relationship with him, which no other creature on earth possesses. The first man lived in an indescribably beautiful garden with everything provided for him until he made the choice to disobey God. By his rebellious choice, he rejected the life God had chosen for him. Rebellion always shouts, "I will do it my way, not yours!" By his own choice, man separated himself from God, from the very presence of the one who desired what was good and best and perfect for him. Man lost his place, his status, his relationship with his Creator. Now, because of Jesus, we have been given the *right* to become God's children. It's our *right,* or opportunity, but with no coercion. God's gift of salvation extends to everyone, but he will not force anyone to accept his offer. However, accepting God's plan of salvation "legally" adopts us into God's family. We become his children.

> *Have you exercised your right to be adopted?*

Is Salvation a Free Gift?

The answer is a resounding YES! Our salvation (redemption) was bought and paid for by Jesus Christ and is offered to us as a gift. We must receive it as a gift. Something you pay for personally is not a gift. Man can never DO enough good works to earn his own salvation; he cannot observe the law perfectly enough. He must depend totally upon God's method for paying for his sin, receiving it by FAITH in Jesus Christ. This gift is made available to us *only* by God's grace.

Eph. 2:8-9

"For it is by *grace* you have been saved, *through faith* – and this not from yourselves, *it is the gift of God* – not by works, so that no one can boast."

Romans 3:22-24

"This righteousness from God comes *through faith in Jesus Christ* to all who believe. There is no difference, for all have sinned and fall short of the glory of God, and are justified freely *by his grace* through the redemption that came by Christ Jesus."

> *Have you been trying to earn God's gift?*

Isn't Salvation Joining the Church?

Salvation is not joining the church or even maintaining our membership. We are not saved by how often we attend church or by how much we give or by how hard we work. We are not eligible for heaven because we are members of a particular denomination or a certain family. We are not accepted by God because we are a "good" person or have lived a "good" life. We cannot buy, barter, earn, or deserve salvation.

Isaiah 64:6
> "All of us have become like one who is unclean, and all our righteous acts are like filthy rags; we all shrivel up like a leaf, and like the wind our sins sweep us away."

Salvation is obtained ONLY through faith in Jesus Christ.

Acts 4:12
> "*Salvation is found in no one else*, for there is no other name under heaven given to men by which we must be saved."

Titus 3:4-7
> "But when the kindness and love of God our Savior appeared, he saved us, *not because of righteous things we had done*, but because of his mercy. He saved us through the washing of rebirth and renewal by the Holy Spirit, whom he poured out on us generously *through Jesus Christ* our Savior, so

that, having been justified by his grace, we might become heirs having the hope of eternal life."

> **Who (or what) are you trusting in for salvation?**

Are There Requirements to Receiving Salvation?

Yes, but not in the sense of earning or deserving it. God's requirements involve acknowledging your inability to save yourself, accepting His gift, and giving Him absolute lordship over your life. This involves:

Repentance - Repentance is a change of one's *mind and will* arising from sorrow for sin and leads to a transformed life (a complete 180). For example, suppose I'm in Texas and my destination is California, but I begin traveling east. Along the way, someone says to me, "You are going the wrong direction to reach California." When I realize they are right, I don't repent that the road signs are wrong or that I am not making any progress toward California. I don't repent that I am in Alabama or that I stopped to eat at the McDonalds in Louisiana instead of New Mexico. No! I acknowledge that my entire direction has been wrong, I repent by making a 180° turnaround, and I begin heading in the right direction. This must be my response to the Gospel. I acknowledge that I have been going in a completely wrong direction, turn totally around, and begin my journey in the right direction.

Repentance was taught by:

<u>John the Baptist</u>: Mark 1:4 and Luke 3:3
<u>Jesus</u>: Mark 1:15, Luke 13:3 and Luke 24:47
<u>The Apostles</u>: Acts 2:38, Acts 3:19, Acts 26:20

<u>Confession</u> - outward confession with our mouth. Oral communication is a gift from God, but most of us don't understand the power of our words. The Bible tells us that "long ago *by God's word* the heavens existed and the earth was formed . . ." (2 Peter 3:5). Jesus told us that "men will have to give account on the day of judgment for every *careless word* they have spoken. For by your words you will be acquitted, and by your words you will be condemned" (Matthew 12:36, 37). *Outward* confession or acknowledgment with the words of our mouth is as important as the *inward* believing with our heart.

Rom. 10:9-10

> "If you *confess with your mouth*, Jesus is Lord, and believe in your heart that God raised him from the dead, you will be saved. For it is with your heart that you believe and are justified, and it is *with your mouth that you confess* and are saved."

Matt. 10:32-33

> "Whoever *acknowledges me* before men, I will also acknowledge him before my Father in heaven. But whoever disowns me before men, I will disown him before my Father in heaven."

<u>Faith</u> - inward belief with your heart. It is believing that what God said is true, that Jesus died to pay for your sins. It is acknowledging that Jesus is the *only* way to be reconciled to God the Father, the *only* way to obtain eternal life.

Rom. 10:9-10
> "If you confess with your mouth, Jesus is Lord, and *believe in your heart* that God raised him from the dead, you will be saved. For it is *with your heart that you believe and are justified*, and it is with your mouth that you confess and are saved."

John 3:14-15
> "Just as Moses lifted up the snake in the desert, so the Son of Man must be lifted up, that *everyone who believes in him* may have eternal life."

I John 5:13
> "I write these things to you *who believe* in the name of the Son of God so that you may know that you have eternal life."

Salvation requires action on both God's part and ours. God has already taken the initiative and his action is primary in salvation.

John 6:44
> "No one can come to me unless *the Father* who sent me *draws him*, and I will raise him up at the last day."

John 6:65
> "This is why I told you that no one can come to me unless the *Father has enabled him*."

Our part is to respond - to believe in the One God sent.

John 6:28-29
> "Then they asked him, 'What must we do to do the works God requires?' Jesus answered, the work of God is this: *to believe in the one he has sent*."

John 6:40

"For my Father's will is that everyone who looks to the Son and *believes in him* shall have eternal life, and I will raise him up at the last day."

In our world today, and especially in America, the idea that "***I** can do it*" pervades our thinking and feeds our egos. How we long and strive to be strong, rich, in control, influential, successful. That's what society demands. That's what impresses others. This attitude often carries over into being able to provide our own way to heaven. If we stack up enough charitable deeds . . . If we become holy enough through spiritual disciplines . . . If we're kind enough or good enough, and on and on. The problem is, how much is enough?

There's nothing wrong with competition or being the best one can be. I admire people who are disciplined and have the ability to perform with finesse, whether musically, academically, or athletically. I believe we should be our best and develop our gifts and talents fully. If the requirements for entering the Kingdom of God rested on any earthly achievement, however, I probably would not qualify. Therefore, it's extremely good news to me that becoming a Christian is not a competition. Human effort is not the qualifier. The same qualifications apply to every person on the face of the earth. One way was made, one price was paid. You and I are equally eligible.

In the same way, many feel totally ineligible because of the life they have lived. They believe they have committed too many sins to be forgiven. They are convinced a holy God would not want anything to do with them. The weight of their past sins rests on their shoulders like a thousand-pound barbell. If good, honest, worthy accomplishments don't qualify one for heaven, neither do the worst sins imaginable disqualify us. One way was made, one price was paid - for everyone!

Romans 5:8
> "But God demonstrates his own love for us in this: *While we were still sinners*, Christ died for us."

> **Have you responded to God by believing in the One he sent?**

<u>Do you know how much God loves you?</u>

So much of what we perceive of God's love has been skewed by what we see around us or know in our own experience. We humans *have love* for others, which is usually conditional upon their response to us. Sometimes we are able to love someone "unlovely" or even an enemy, but that is certainly the exception. Most of the time we don't even *like* such people, much less love them. Tolerate is a better word.

But God's love isn't like ours. God doesn't *have* love – He *IS* love. Love is part of His nature. His love is pure and unconditional, not flawed with expectations or blemished by feelings or whims. His love is so far above ours that it is hard to comprehend. His love gives with no expectation of return. His love reaches out and embraces even the most unlovely among us.

John 3:16
> "For God *so loved the world* that he gave his one and only Son, that whoever believes in him shall not perish but have eternal life."

Ephesians 2:4-5
> "But because of his *great love for us*, God, who is rich in mercy, made us alive with Christ even when we

were dead in transgressions – it is by grace you have been saved."

1 John 4:9-11

"This is how God showed his love among us: He sent his one and only Son into the world that we might live through him. This is love; not that we loved God, but that *he loved us* and sent his Son as an atoning sacrifice for our sins. Dear friends, since God so loved us, we also ought to love one another."

Most people struggle with the concept that God could love them *unconditionally*. We may feel we have done too many "bad" things or strayed too far away for God to love us. At times in my own life, the enemy persistently tried to convince me I had somehow, in some way, committed the "unpardonable sin" and God would never forgive me. When I met obstacles or problems, I felt God was punishing me. When I didn't get answers to prayers right away or the ones I expected, I took that as a sign He was mad at me. I lived largely by my feelings rather than the truth. God used a Bible teacher, Malcolm Smith (no relation), to help me understand the all-encompassing, unconditional, everlasting, and outrageous love the Father has for us – for me and you. Embracing truth radically changed my life. Accepting His love brought the peace and joy for which I longed and gave me an entirely new perspective. Romans 8:28 (Message Bible) states, "That's why we can be so sure that every detail in our lives of love for God is worked into something good." He takes the bad and makes something good take place in us and for us.

> *Are you allowing God to pour His love into your life?*

What's Next?

Salvation is the <u>initial</u> step in becoming a child of God. We are "born again" by the Spirit of God into God's family through faith in His Son Jesus Christ. We were bought and paid for -- the price was the precious blood of Jesus -- and when we obtain salvation, we become his possession. We no longer belong to ourselves.

I Cor. 6:19-20
> "You are not your own; you were bought at a price."

(See also Acts 20:28 and 1 Cor. 7:23)

<u>Baptism in water</u> is the next step. Jesus set the example for water baptism when he was baptized by John the Baptist in the Jordan River. Even though Jesus did not need to repent, he fully met all the righteous requirements of God including baptism.

Matt. 3:15
> Jesus said to John, ". . . it is proper for us to do this (be baptized) to fulfill all righteousness."

In the last command Jesus gave his disciples just before his ascension, known as the Great Commission, he told them to baptize those who had become disciples in every nation.

Matt. 28:19-20
> "Therefore go and make disciples of all nations, *baptizing them in the name of the Father and of the Son and of the Holy Spirit*, and teaching them to obey everything I have commanded you. And surely I am with you always, to the very end of the age."

Baptism follows repentance and is an act of obedience. It is a symbolic demonstration that one has identified himself with Christ in his death, burial, and resurrection.

Acts 2:38

> "Peter replied, *Repent and be baptized*, every one of you, in the name of Jesus Christ for the forgiveness of your sins. And you will receive the gift of the Holy Spirit."

Just as circumcision was a sign in the Israelite community that the individual was in covenant relationship with God, so water baptism is the parallel sign that the Christian stands in covenant relationship with Jesus Christ.

Col. 2:11-12

> "In him you were also circumcised, in the putting off of the sinful nature, not with a circumcision done by the hands of men but with the circumcision done by Christ, having been *buried with him in baptism and raised with him through your faith in the power of God*, who raised him from the dead."

In a number of churches, infant baptism is practiced. The church we attended when our sons were born believed that children should be presented to the Lord at a young age. The parents took vows, promising to teach their children about God and bring them up in conformity to the Word of God. The parents also were to encourage their children to make a profession of faith at the appropriate time, when they were old enough to understand making a commitment of their life to the Lord. We had our sons baptized when they were only a few months old and dedicated them to the Lord. Later, after they had accepted Christ as Savior, they were both baptized by immersion. The need for each individual to be baptized in water should certainly follow making a decision to become a follower of Jesus. Not only is baptism an act of obedience, it is an outward sign to the community of believers and the world that he identifies and now stands in covenant relationship with Christ.

> *Have you been baptized?*

Many people think they can stop here, but that is not what the Bible teaches. Today, people are looking for a low-maintenance, low-cost remedy – something easy, a quick fix, something that requires little or no commitment. We want a contract for "fire insurance" to keep us out of hell without a relationship with Jesus Christ. However, there is no such thing as salvation without a relationship – a *covenant* relationship. It is at this point that we falter. Our western culture has no true understanding of making a covenant with someone. Even the marriage covenant today has no real meaning, and we break covenant with little concern for the consequences. However, God's covenant relationship with mankind is a central theme throughout the Bible resulting in either life or death, blessings or curses.

Exploring Salvation

Chapter 5

A Covenant Relationship

According to *Webster's New World Dictionary*, 2nd College Edition, a covenant is a formal, solemn, and binding agreement between two or more parties, especially for the performance of some action, also referred to as a pledge or a compact. Today, we refer to a covenant as a contract which has terms or requirements that must be upheld by both parties. Such a covenant is legally binding and results in penalties or consequences for those who break it.

In biblical times, the implications for breaking covenant were so severe that Jesus warned his followers in Luke 14:28-33 to "count the cost." The Greek word *diatheke* referred to a binding will made by a person to ensure the proper disposal of his possessions after his death, his last will and testament. In the New Testament this word was translated "covenant." The Hebrew word for testament is *berith* and is also translated "covenant." When you understand covenant you will begin to understand the Bible and the message of both the Old and New Testaments or covenants.

Covenant is the very foundation of the Bible, a concept God himself introduced. Throughout Scripture we are given glimpses of the Everlasting Covenant made before time began in eternity between the Godhead – Father, Son and Holy Spirit – which declared the eternal purpose for man involving both creation and redemption. We are given glimpses of the Everlasting Covenant which are woven through the covenants God made with man.

Genesis 9:16

> "Whenever the rainbow appears in the clouds, I will see it and remember the *everlasting covenant* between God and all living creatures of every kind on the earth."

Isaiah 55:3

> "I will make an *everlasting covenant* with you, my faithful love promised to David."

Heb. 13:20

> "May the God of peace, who through the blood of the *eternal covenant* brought back from the dead our Lord Jesus . . ."

In the Old Testament, God entered into covenant with:

- Adam (Genesis 3) and Noah (Genesis 9), which included all mankind and all creatures.

- Abraham (Genesis 12, 15 & 17), Moses (Exodus 19-24) and David (2 Samuel 7), which involved His chosen nation of Israel.

The New Testament or New Covenant was the culmination of the Old Testament covenants through their promised Messiah, the Christ, and includes all who choose to enter into a relationship with Christ Jesus. This was prophesied by Jeremiah about 600 years before its fulfillment.

Jer. 31:31-34

> "The time is coming," declares the Lord, "when I will make a *new covenant* with the house of Israel and with the house of Judah. It will not be like the covenant I made with their forefathers when I took them by the hand to lead them out of Egypt, because they broke my covenant, though I was a

A Covenant Relationship

husband to them," declares the Lord. "This is the covenant I will make with the house of Israel after that time," declares the Lord. "I will put my law in their minds and write it on their hearts. I will be their God, and they will be my people. No longer will a man teach his neighbor, or a man his brother, saying, 'know the Lord,' because they will all know me, from the least of them to the greatest," declares the Lord. "For I will forgive their wickedness and will remember their sins no more."

When two parties entered a covenant relationship, witnesses were called to ensure accountability to the covenant agreement. The ancient ritual of covenant-making was called "cutting a covenant," in which a sacrificial animal was cut in half and the pieces placed on the ground. During the ceremony the two parties would walk between the pieces of this animal called the "walk of death." There was always an exchange of robes, weapons, and belts, followed by a meal. The participants were saying to the other, "I am giving myself to you – my identity, my rights, my enemies, my possessions, my debts, my strengths, my weaknesses – and I freely take your identity, your rights, your enemies, your possessions, your debts, your strengths and your weaknesses. What I have is yours and what you have is mine. We are one."

This is *exactly* what Jesus did for us – he exchanged his divinity for our humanity, his sinlessness for our sinfulness, his power for our weakness. He "cut a covenant" with His own precious blood and took the "walk of death" for our redemption.

Philippians 2:6-8

"Who, being in very nature God, did not consider equality with God something to be grasped, but made himself nothing, taking the very nature of a servant, being made in human likeness. And being found in appearance as a man, he humbled himself and became obedient to death – even death on a cross."

Our walk of death involves dying to self so that God can be everything to us and in us. It is a vow to die to all independent living, all idols, all self-righteousness, all self-seeking, all self-love. We belong to God, so "self" must be removed from the throne of our life and Jesus Christ enthroned there. We are pledging faithfulness, loyalty, and obedience to Him.

Romans 6:1-2

> "What shall we say, then? Shall we go on sinning so that grace may increase? By no means! *We died to sin*; how can we live in it any longer?"

Colossians 3:5-6

> "*Put to death*, therefore, whatever belongs to your earthly nature: sexual immorality, impurity, lust, evil desires and greed, which is idolatry. Because of these, the wrath of God is coming."

(See also 1 Peter 2:24 and Colossians 3:2-3)

The robe represents the exchange of our garment of sin (the sinful, fleshly nature) for Jesus' robe of righteousness. I will no longer wear mine, but His. Jesus was made sin for us so that we could become righteous "in him."

2 Cor. 5:21

> "God made him (Jesus) who had no sin to be sin for us, so that in him we might become the righteousness of God."

Isaiah 61:10

> "For he has clothed me with garments of salvation and arrayed me in a robe of righteousness . . ."

(See also Romans 13:14)

A Covenant Relationship

The exchange of <u>weapons</u> represents our receiving God's weapons of warfare and His covenant promises to fight for us. We are promised victory over the power of sin in our lives and over the schemes of the devil to destroy us. Jesus came to destroy Satan's power.

1 John 3:8
>"The reason the Son of God appeared was to destroy the devil's work."

2 Cor. 10:4
>"The weapons we fight with are not the weapons of the world. On the contrary, they have divine power to demolish strongholds."

Exodus 14:14
>"The Lord will fight for you; you need only to be still."

Ephesians 6:11
>"Put on the full armor of God so that you can take your stand against the devil's schemes."

The <u>belt</u> was used to hold a person's weapons and represents an exchange of strength. God gives us His strength in exchange for our inadequacy, His power for our weakness. None of God's resources will be withheld from us.

2 Cor. 12:9
>"My grace is sufficient for you, for my power is made perfect in weakness."

Philippians 4:13
>"I can do everything through him who gives me strength."

Philippians 4:19
> "And my God will meet all your needs according to his glorious riches in Christ Jesus."

Sharing a <u>meal</u> was the culmination of cutting a covenant with another and involved both breaking bread and drinking wine, representing the shed blood of the sacrificial animal. The participants were expressing their willingness to have their bodies broken and their blood shed for one another; even if this should happen, the covenant would never be broken. Now we can understand the significance of the Lord's Supper, also called the Eucharist or Communion, that Jesus instructed his followers to celebrate. Each time we participate in this ordinance, we are actually renewing our covenant with God and with one another.

Luke 22:19-20
> "And he (Jesus) took bread, gave thanks and broke it, and gave it to them, saying, 'This is my body given for you; do this in remembrance of me.' In the same way, after the supper he took the cup, saying, 'This cup is the new covenant in my blood, which is poured out for you.'"

John 6:53
> Jesus said to them, "I tell you the truth, unless you eat the flesh of the Son of Man and drink his blood, you have no life in you."

There was a dual purpose for God's covenants: (a) to convey to mankind his will and purpose for creating him, and (b) to provide a way to redeem mankind after he sinned. Man was the crowning glory of God's creation and God desired a relationship with man, but this was impossible apart from covenant. Therefore, God initiated the covenants and swore by his own holiness to keep the covenants he had made. We can count on their fulfillment down to the last detail. God cannot lie! Man, however, is another story. Even though man was made in the image of God, he was given a free will to accept or reject a relationship with his Creator. Over and over in the Old Testament we see the utter bankruptcy of man as he chooses to break covenant. We still have that choice.

Every Old Testament covenant, mediated by the Levitical priests, pointed to Jesus Christ, who became our High Priest. This covenant was made for us. In fact, Jesus said, "This is my body, which is *for you*" (1 Corinthians 11:24). This New Covenant in Jesus Christ is the very foundation upon which a Christian's life is built. It is the basis for his ability to live in obedience to God, to bear good fruit, and to love God will all his heart. There are several aspects to the New Covenant we need to understand.

Jesus is the fulfillment and mediator of the New Covenant

Luke 22:20

"In the same way, after the supper he took the cup, saying, 'This cup is *the new covenant in my blood*, which is poured out for you.'"

Hebrews 8:6

"But the ministry Jesus has received is as superior to theirs (the high priests) as the covenant *of which he is mediator* is superior to the old one, and it is founded on better promises."

Hebrews 9:15

"For this reason *Christ is the mediator of a new covenant*, that those who are called may receive the promised eternal inheritance—now that he has died as a ransom to set them free from the sins committed under the first covenant."

(See also Isaiah 42:6; and Deuteronomy 30:11-14)

A Covenant Relationship

<u>The Holy Spirit was given to us as a covenant promise</u>.

It is impossible to walk in a covenant relationship with God without the empowering of the Holy Spirit. That is the very reason the Holy Spirit was given to us. This is covered in more detail in Chapter 6.

Romans 8:13
> "For if you live according to the sinful nature, you will die; but if *by the Spirit* you put to death the misdeeds of the body, you will live."

2 Cor. 1:21-22
> "Now it is God who makes both us and you stand firm in Christ. He anointed us, set his seal of ownership on us, and *put his Spirit in our hearts* as a deposit, guaranteeing what is to come."

(See also Acts 1:4-5)

<u>Sin breaks covenant with God</u>.

Not necessarily *a* sin, but the choice to *continue* sinning in one or more areas with an *unrepentant* heart breaks covenant with God. Genuine repentance turns one *away* from that sin, breaks the stronghold over his life, and firmly establishes the lordship of Jesus. A divided heart is one not *fully committed* to Jesus Christ. We are all tempted to sin, but a divided heart chooses to please his fleshly desires over choosing to please God, whether idols or lusts or unbelief. Faithful obedience to God is walking in covenant.

Hosea 6:7
> "Like Adam, they have broken the covenant–they were unfaithful to me there."

A Covenant Relationship

Josh. 24:14a, 15
> "Now fear the Lord and serve him with all faithfulness. But if serving the Lord seems undesirable to you, then choose for yourselves this day whom you will serve . . ."

Isaiah 59:2
> "But your iniquities have separated you from your God; your sins have hidden his face from you, so that he will not hear."

Are there still consequences for breaking covenant?

Deuteronomy 28 lists the blessings for obedience and the curses for disobedience under the Mosaic Covenant. We are no longer justified or made holy by observing the customs, ordinances, and rituals of the Mosaic Law. We are declared righteous by what Christ Jesus has done that the law could not do. We are now under grace and enjoy a new freedom in Christ Jesus.

Romans 10:4
> "Christ is the end of the law so that there may be righteousness for everyone who believes."

Romans 3:21-22
> "But now a righteousness from God, apart from law, has been made known, to which the Law and the Prophets testify. This righteousness from God comes through faith in Jesus Christ to all who believe."

However, we are *not* free from the Law of Christ which is written in our hearts. God's righteous requirements have not changed. Grace does not excuse sin or eliminate obedience.

A Covenant Relationship

Romans 3:31
> "Do we, then, nullify the law by this faith? Not at all! Rather, we uphold the law."

Romans 6:1-2
> "What shall we say, then? Shall we go on sinning so that grace may increase? By no means! We died to sin; how can we live in it any longer?"

Matthew 5:17
> "Do not think that I have come to abolish the Law or the Prophets; I have not come to abolish them but to fulfill them."

(See also Romans 6:15)

No person who walks in sincere love, obedience, and repentance before God falls under His wrath. However, those who refuse to obey the Law of Christ in their hearts and choose to walk in rebellion, fall under the judgment and wrath of Almighty God.

John 3:36
> "Whoever believes in the Son has eternal life, but whoever rejects the Son will not see life, for God's wrath remains on him."

Romans 1:18
> "The wrath of God is being revealed from heaven against all the godlessness and wickedness of men who suppress the truth by their wickedness."

Romans 2:5
> "But because of your stubbornness and your unrepentant heart, you are storing up wrath against yourself for the day of God's wrath, when his righteous judgment will be revealed."

A Covenant Relationship

<u>Are there conditions to maintaining this covenant relationship?</u>

The answer is YES! Just as in a marriage covenant, there are not only expectations each partner has of the other, there are also conditions and requirements in maintaining the relationship. No relationship can thrive unless both parties are fully involved. So it is in our relationship with Jesus Christ -- the Bible is clear on the requirements.

<u>Obedience</u>

Heb. 5:8-9
> "Although he was a son, he learned obedience from what he suffered and, once made perfect, he became the source of eternal salvation *for all who obey him*."

John 14:21
> "Whoever has my commands and *obeys them*, he is the one who loves me. He who loves me will be loved by my Father, and I too will love him and show myself to him."

Matt. 7:21
> "Not everyone who says to me, Lord, Lord, will enter the kingdom of heaven, but only he who *does the will* of my Father who is in heaven." (Also read verses 22-23)

<u>Remain/Abide</u>

John 15:9-10
> "As the Father has loved me, so have I loved you. Now *remain in my love*. If you *obey* my commands, you will *remain in my love*, just as I have obeyed my Father's commands and remain in his love."

A Covenant Relationship

1 John 2:24-25
> "See that what you have heard from the beginning *remains in you. If it does, you also will remain in the Son and in the Father.* And this is what he promised us -- even eternal life."

(See also John 15:1, 2, and 4)

Continue

Col. 1:22-23
> "But now he has reconciled you by Christ's physical body through death to present you holy in his sight, without blemish and free from accusation -- *if you continue in your faith*, established and firm, not moved from the hope held out in the gospel."

Rom. 11:22
> "Consider therefore the kindness and sternness of God: sternness to those who fell, but kindness to you, provided that you *continue in his kindness*. Otherwise, you also will be cut off."

Follow

John 10:27-29
> "My sheep listen to my voice; I know them, and *they follow me*. I give them eternal life, and they shall never perish; no one can snatch them out of my hand. My Father, who has given them to me, is greater than all; no one can snatch them out of my Father's hand."

Do what is right

I John 2:29
> "If you know that he is righteous, you know that everyone who *does what is right* has been born of him."

Titus 2:14
> "(Christ) gave himself for us to redeem us from all wickedness and to purify for himself a people that are his very own, eager to *do what is good.*"

> *Are you living in a true covenant relationship with Jesus Christ?*

We are not signing a contract for salvation; we're entering into a covenant. The terms of a contract indicate a designated length of time in which the contract will be in effect. Covenants are different and indicate a long-term commitment, not a designated date of expiration. The marriage covenant is 'til death'; God's covenant is for eternity. Just as in marriage, the wedding *event* is merely the beginning of a lifelong journey together. It marks the start date. The same is true for salvation. The initial event for a new Christian is the moment he/she accepts God's gift of salvation, which launches a lifelong commitment to a relationship with Jesus Christ.

A Covenant Relationship

Chapter 6

Ready for the Adventure

Our life in Christ has been described as a journey, a race, a walk, an ongoing process. The Bible describes it as a time in which we grow in grace, bear fruit for righteousness, develop spiritual maturity, and learn to be an overcomer. Of necessity there is a starting point for any journey; so it is with salvation. The moment we accept Jesus Christ as our Savior and Lord, we begin a new life, enter an incredible relationship with our Creator, and start an awesome adventure. An interesting Scripture in Philippians gives further insight into this continuing journey.

Phil. 2:12-13

> "Therefore, my dear friends, as you have always obeyed -- not only in my presence, but now much more in my absence -- *continue to work out your salvation with fear and trembling,* for it is God who works in you to will and to act according to his good purpose."

How do we "work out our salvation"? I thought salvation was a free gift? Is this a contradiction? No, it is not a contradiction; salvation through Jesus Christ is definitely a free gift and cannot be earned, deserved or purchased. The last part of that verse clarifies the meaning for us. God is working *in us* to bring about *His purposes*. However, we still have a choice: to allow Him to bring about needed changes in our lives, or to rebel and resist Him. Herein lies our work – to submit or to resist.

Ephesians 2:10 tells us that "we are God's workmanship, created in Christ Jesus to do good works." In the Greek the idea of workmanship is conveyed as a "work of art." We are God's work of art, a work in progress. God is the artist, the craftsman who has a design, a purpose, a plan in mind for each of us. Our part is to give Him permission to change us, to mold us as a potter molds the clay, into the image of Jesus Christ. What if the clay jumped off the potter's wheel and declared its independence from the potter saying, "I don't understand what you are doing to me. I would rather mold myself into the vessel I think I should be." That piece of clay would never become what the potter intended and would probably end up a mess. You are not a group project, not one of a cluster. You are an original, one-of-a-kind, unique, and God will work in *you* what *you* need in order to form *you* into that beautiful person he designed *you* to be.

Sometimes the Potter's hand is pleasant . . . sometimes it isn't. But God always works for your *good*. Philippians 1:6 tells us "that He who has begun a *good* work in you will perform it until the day of Jesus Christ." Romans 8:28 states, "And we know that in all things God works for the *good* of those who love him, who have been called according to his purpose." Two things in this verse are important to notice. First, he is speaking to those who have chosen to give their lives to Christ. Those living in rebellion to God continue to be the center of their own lives. They are actually allowing the "god of this world" to control their thinking and desires and decisions. Therefore, all things probably are NOT working for their good. Second, it says that God works for our *good*. The "good" is that which conforms our character to the likeness of His Son; it is that which saves us from our own selfish ambitions and directs us to His purposes for our lives. The "good" transforms our thinking; it changes wrong desires; it replaces anxiety and fear; it brings true satisfaction, peace, and joy in our daily living. Sometimes it is hard to see the "good" that God is working out because we are so focused on the "all things" that constantly bombard us. God's ultimate desire for His children is that we trust Him enough to look *through* the "things" – the situations and difficulties – and see Him at work in all the happenings we face.

Many times when situations don't work out as planned or answers to our prayers are delayed, we are hurt and disappointed. The biggest lesson here is that an omniscient God knew that the end result would ultimately have led to disaster. It wasn't what was best. We do not understand that God is ALL KNOWING and ALL LOVING and ALWAYS and in ALL WAYS working for our good. Because we cannot see the bigger picture, we react in anger and frustration, blaming God of "child abuse." We react like a little two-year-old who throws a temper tantrum because he didn't get what he wanted. In the example of the potter and clay, the potter cannot mold the clay if it isn't pliable. To be pliable means to completely abandon ourselves to the Potter. Preconceived ideas of our own design and plan must be submitted to God. We must trust the Potter even when we cannot see the purpose for what is happening.

To submit or not submit – that is the question. Learning submission to His will *in every area* is worked out through daily walking with God, learning to hear and recognize His voice, establishing our intimate relationship with Him, and choosing to be obedient. God will do the work *in us* as we submit to Him. Total submission to God will bring about the death of "self." That's what "dying to self" is – bringing your will and desires into line with God's will and plan for your life. As you desire God's will to totally dominate your life, you will find your own selfish desires and will changing, until all you want is God. Psalm 37:4 promises that if you delight yourself in the Lord, he will give you the desires of your heart. In other words, he will give you the desires you should have. And that brings us full circle to what sin is – SELF living independently of God.

Another term used in Scripture, which is synonymous with "working out one's salvation," is to "make one's calling and election sure." One doesn't just get his foot in the door of heaven, so to speak, and then stop there. Salvation isn't simply a "happening" or a "get it and forget it" gift that one can stuff into some remote part of his life. Salvation is entering into a *covenant relationship* with Jesus Christ and is a *commitment* to maintain that relationship. This commitment involves growing in knowledge, understanding and wisdom of God through his Word and prayer, continual change in our behavior and lifestyle, loving others through our words and actions, and much more. The Good News is that God also gives us the ability to live a life that pleases Him through the power of the Holy Spirit. We are not left to struggle on our own and end up defeated. <u>Absolutely not!</u>

2 Peter 1:3-11

> "His divine power (the Holy Spirit) has given us everything we need for life and godliness through our knowledge of him who called us by his own glory and goodness. Through these he has given us his very great and precious promises, so that through them you may participate in the divine nature and escape the corruption in the world caused by evil desires. For this very reason, make every effort to add to your faith goodness; and to goodness, knowledge; and to knowledge, self-control; and to self-control, perseverance; and to perseverance, godliness; and to godliness, brotherly kindness; and to brotherly kindness, love. For if you possess these qualities in increasing measure, they will keep you from being ineffective and unproductive in your knowledge of our Lord Jesus Christ. But if anyone does not have them, he is nearsighted and blind, and has forgotten that he has been cleansed from his past sins. Therefore, my brothers, be all the more eager to *make your calling and election sure*. For if you do these things, you will never fall, and you will receive a rich welcome into the eternal kingdom of our Lord and Savior Jesus Christ."

Being "born again" is the beginning of a process, not an end in itself. Salvation is the starting point of an incredible journey.

Much like the birth of a human baby, a new life is launched on a journey of learning, growing, and eventually developing into a mature adult. If a baby isn't growing, changing, and maturing, we become alarmed – something is very wrong! So, too, we should expect change and growth into mature Christians.

1 Peter 2:2-3
> "Like newborn babies, crave pure spiritual milk, so that by it you may *grow up in your salvation*, now that you have tasted that the Lord is good."

(See also Hebrews 5:11-14 and 2 Thessalonians 1:3)

> *Are you working out your salvation by giving God permission to make needed changes in you?*

Our God, Creator of the Universe, has the full set of plans; everything was prepared in advance. The only thing that hinders His work in our lives is our resistance or rebellion. When we give him full permission to continue his "work of art" in us, the Holy Spirit will faithfully and gently begin that molding process, removing the sin blemishes and creating the beautiful life he designed for us.

Who is the Holy Spirit?

The Holy Spirit is a person and not an influence; He is the third person of the Trinity. Jesus told his disciples to "go and make disciples of all the nations, baptizing them in the name of the

Father and of the Son and of the Holy Spirit" (Matthew 28:19). He is seen from the very first verses of Genesis where it says that "the Spirit of God was hovering over the face of the waters" (Gen. 1:2), to the closing verses of Revelation with the benediction, "And the Spirit and the bride say, 'Come!'" (Rev. 22:17).

In the Old Testament, the Holy Spirit was given to individuals to empower them for specific responsibilities or service. Over and over it states that "the Spirit of the Lord came upon" individuals such as Daniel, Gideon, Samson, Saul, David and others. The prophets of old, who were the spokespersons for God in conveying His word to the people, are described as being "carried along by the Holy Spirit" (2 Peter 1:20-21).

In the New Testament the Holy Spirit was made available to all. He is seen as God present and active in the lives of individuals. He has been described as the "breath" of God, wind, fire, and power. On the day of Pentecost, He was heard as a "mighty rushing wind" and seen as "tongues of fire" on the hundred and twenty followers of Jesus assembled, probably in the temple court area. He is called the Spirit of Truth (John 14:17), Teacher (Luke 12:12), Helper (John 15:26), Counselor/Comforter (John 14:16, 26), and Witness (Romans 8:16). Jesus referred to the Holy Spirit as "streams of living water" in John 7:38-39. He was sent to teach, lead, guide, convict, give life, bring things to our remembrance, give discernment, make Jesus known, and enable us to live a life pleasing to God.

<u>He is the promised gift of the Father</u>.

Acts 1:4-5

> "Do not leave Jerusalem, but wait for the gift my Father promised, which you have heard me speak about. For John baptized with water, but in a few days you will be baptized with the Holy Spirit."

(See also Joel 2:28-29 and Luke 11:13)

<u>His work is primary in salvation.</u>

John 3:5-8

> Jesus answered, "I tell you the truth, no one can enter the kingdom of God unless he is born of water and *the Spirit*. Flesh gives birth to flesh, but *the Spirit gives birth to spirit*. You should not be surprised at my saying, 'You must be born again.' The wind blows wherever it pleases. You hear its sound, but you cannot tell where it comes from or where it is going. So it is with everyone *born of the Spirit*."

Titus 3:5-6

> "He saved us, not because of righteous things we had done, but because of his mercy. He saved us through the washing of rebirth and renewal *by the Holy Spirit*, whom he poured out on us generously through Jesus Christ our Savior."

<u>He witnesses to who Jesus is.</u>

John 15:26

> "When the Counselor comes, whom I will send to you from the Father, the Spirit of truth who goes out from the Father, he will testify about me."

<u>He indwells believers; our bodies are His temple.</u>

Ephesians 2:22

> "And in him you too are being built together to become a dwelling in which *God lives by his Spirit*."

1 Cor. 3:16-17

> "Don't you know that yourselves are God's temple and that *God's Spirit lives in you?* If anyone destroys God's temple, God will destroy him; for God's temple is sacred, and you are that temple."

(See also Romans 8:11; John 14:16-17; Romans 8:9; 1 Cor. 6:19-20)

<u>He teaches us.</u>

John 14:26

> "But the counselor, the Holy Spirit, whom the Father will send in my name, will *teach you* all things and will *remind you* of everything I have said to you."

<u>He empowers for service.</u>

Acts 1:8

> "But *you will receive power* when the Holy Spirit comes on you; and you will be my witnesses in Jerusalem, and in all Judea and Samaria, and to the ends of the earth."

Luke 24:49b

> "But stay in the city until you have been *clothed with power* from on high."

<u>He intercedes for us.</u>

Romans 8:26-27

> "In the same way, the Spirit helps us in our weakness. We do not know what we ought to pray for, but *the Spirit himself intercedes for us* with groans that words cannot express. And he who searches our hearts knows the mind of the Spirit because *the*

Spirit intercedes for the saints in accordance with God's will."

He enables us to overcome sin.

Romans 8:13-14
"For if you live according to the sinful nature, you will die; but if *by the Spirit* you put to death the misdeeds of the body, you will live, because those who are led by the Spirit of God are sons of God."

Galatians 5:16
"So I say, live by the Spirit, and you will not gratify the desires of the sinful nature."

He produces fruit in our lives.

Galatians 5:22-23
"But the *fruit of the Spirit* is love, joy, peace, patience, kindness, goodness, faithfulness, gentleness and self-control."

He gives spiritual gifts.

1 Cor. 12:4, 7-11
"There are different kinds of gifts, but the same Spirit. Now to each one the manifestation of the Spirit is given for the common good. To one there is given through the Spirit the message of wisdom, to another the message of knowledge, by means of the same Spirit, to another faith by the same Spirit, to another gifts of healing by that one Spirit, to another miraculous powers, to another prophecy, to another distinguishing between spirits, to another speaking in different kinds of tongues, and to still another the interpretation of tongues. All

these are the work of one and the same Spirit, and he gives them to each one, just as he determines."

Warnings concerning the Holy Spirit.

1 Thess. 5:19-20
"Do not put out the Spirit's fire; do not treat prophecies with contempt."

Ephesians 4:30
"And do not grieve the Holy Spirit of God, with whom you were sealed for the day of redemption."

Isaiah 63:10
"Yet they rebelled and grieved his Holy Spirit. So he turned and became their enemy and he himself fought against them."

Matt. 12:31-32
"And so I tell you, every sin and blasphemy will be forgiven men, but the blasphemy against the Spirit will not be forgiven. Anyone who speaks a word against the Son of Man will be forgiven, but anyone who speaks against the Holy Spirit will not be forgiven, either in this age or in the age to come."

The above warnings are very strong, so let's look at them in context. Blaspheming is not a word we use often today. *Webster's New World Dictionary*, Second College Edition, defines blasphemy as: "profane or contemptuous speech, writing, or action concerning God or anything held as divine." The setting in which Jesus made the statement in Matthew 12 (also see Mark 3:28-30) was after a demon-possessed man, who was blind and mute, had been brought to Jesus and he healed him. The Pharisees began accusing Jesus of performing this miracle by the power of Beelzebub (Satan). Bible scholars generally agree that this "unpardonable sin" is attributing Jesus' miracles, which were a work of the Holy Spirit, to the work of Satan.

The Holy Spirit is the One who draws us to the Father (see John 6:44). The Holy Spirit is the one who witnesses with our spirit that we belong to God, that we are His children (see Romans 8:16). He is the Spirit of Truth. If one rejects the authenticity of the Spirit of God giving testimony to Jesus through the miracles he does, there is nothing left. The *Message Bible* puts it this way: "There's nothing done or said that can't be forgiven. But if you deliberately persist in your slanders against God's Spirit, you are repudiating the very One who forgives. If you reject the Son of Man out of some misunderstanding, the Holy Spirit can forgive you, but when you reject the Holy Spirit, you're sawing off the branch on which you're sitting, severing by your own perversity all connection with the One who forgives."

The work of the Holy Spirit is primary in the life of an individual, not only to draw him to God, but to enable him to live a Christian life. When you receive Christ as your savior, the Holy Spirit actually marks you as His with a seal. "Having believed, you were marked in him with a seal, the promised Holy Spirit, who is a deposit guaranteeing our inheritance until the redemption of those who are God's possession – to the praise of his glory" (Ephesians 1:13b, 14). He seals you and *guarantees* your inheritance as a child of God.

> *Are you allowing the Holy Spirit to empower your life?*

Ready for the Adventure

Chapter 7

Being Sure of My Destiny

The question of being eternally secure has been scrutinized and seriously debated over the centuries, with varying opinions. To find the answer, we must look carefully at what God's Word says. The Bible clearly states that no person or power under heaven can snatch us away from Jesus Christ or the Father.

John 10:27-29
> "My sheep listen to my voice; I know them, and they follow me. I give them eternal life, and they shall never perish; *no one can snatch them out of my hand.* My Father, who has given them to me, is greater than all; *no one can snatch them out of my Father's hand.*"

But somewhere, sometime in our journey we will have occasion to question our faith. Doubts as to the reality of our salvation may enter our minds. Life happens and we may wonder where God is in all this. These are the times when we must persevere and not lose our confidence.

Heb. 10:35-36,39
> "So do not throw away your confidence; it will be richly rewarded. You need to persevere so that *when you have done the will of God*, you will receive what he has promised. But we are not of those who *shrink back and are destroyed*, but of those who *believe and are saved.*" (Selected verses)

Notice there is a warning with the admonition to persevere. There are two options – to shrink back and be destroyed or to believe and be saved. Again, it is our choice. We are secure in the arms of God, eternally secure, as long as we *continue in our faith* and *abide in Christ*. And that is what salvation is – being IN CHRIST. But God will never force anyone against his will to remain in Christ. It would be strictly by our own choice to turn away from God's provision for salvation or abandon our faith.

1 Timothy 4:1

> "The Spirit clearly says that in later times some will *abandon the faith* and follow deceiving spirits and things taught by demons."

2 Peter 3:17-18

> "Be on your guard so that you may not be carried away by the error of lawless men, and *fall from your secure position*. But grow in the grace and knowledge of our Lord and Savior Jesus Christ."

God desires for *everyone* to be saved. That was his plan from the very beginning. He predestined (or elected) *all* mankind to live eternally with him, and his invitation is to "whosoever" will come. Jesus died for "whosoever" would believe in him (John 3:16). But it's our choice. As someone once said, there are only the whosoeverwills and the whosoeverwon'ts.

God has provided only one way to be saved – by believing in what Jesus Christ has done for us through his death and resurrection. That's it! If his provision is rejected, there is nothing left – there is no Plan B. The following warning is given to those who have been enlightened about salvation, tasted the magnificent gift that God offers, shared in the Holy Spirit, and then turned away. Perhaps this warning is based on what happened with the Israelites en route to the Promised Land. They had experienced the divine leadership, miracles, and blessings of God, but refused to trust God to take them all the way to the promised destination. When the spies brought an evil report of "giants" in the land and obstacles to be overcome, they lost heart and turned away. Absolutely nothing had changed on God's part – he had a plan, he had made them a promise, and he would take them all the way. *They* made the choice to quit believing that God was their deliverer. They gave up their only hope for salvation. All the unbelievers died in the desert and never saw the promise. So will we unless we continue to trust God.

Hebrews 6:4-6

> "It is impossible for those who have once been enlightened, who have tasted the heavenly gift, who have shared in the Holy Spirit, who have tasted the goodness of the word of God and the powers of the coming age, *if they fall away*, to be brought back to repentance, because to their loss they are crucifying the Son of God all over again and subjecting him to public disgrace."

Some believe that those who "fall away" were never genuinely born again, and that may be the case. Only God knows our hearts; that is not for us to judge. But again, the Scriptures are clear that we must continue in our faith.

Col. 1:22-23

> "But now he has reconciled you by Christ's physical body through death to present you holy in his sight, without blemish and free from accusation -- *if you continue in your faith*, established and firm, not moved from the hope held out in the gospel."

In the book of Revelation, there are seven letters written to seven different churches. In each letter is a promise to those who overcome. What does it mean to overcome? *Webster's New World Dictionary*, Second College Edition, states: "To get the better of in competition, struggle, etc.; to conquer, to master, prevail over, or surmount; to be victorious, win." Mastering, prevailing, winning: all imply perseverance, the resolve to finish, and a determination to get the prize.

So it is with continuing our walk with Christ: the <u>resolve</u> is to finish the race of life with Christ; the <u>struggle</u> is the sin and self that wants to dominate; the <u>prize</u> is spending eternity in heaven instead of hell. It is interesting that the promise to the overcomer in Revelation 3:5 is to have ones name *not removed* from the book of life. One's name has to be *in* the book of life in order to be blotted out. Your name was written there when you became a Christian, a believer in Jesus Christ. The importance of having ones name in the book of life is stated in Revelation 20:15, "If anyone's name was *not* found written in the book of life, he was thrown into the lake of fire."

Revelation 3:5

> "He who overcomes will, like them, be dressed in white. I will *never blot out his name* from the book of life, but will acknowledge his name before my Father and his angels."

(See also Exodus 32:32-33.)

In Luke 8:5-8, Jesus told a parable about a farmer sowing seed. Some seeds fell along the path and was trampled on; the birds came and ate it up. Some fell on rock, grew into plants, but quickly withered because there was no moisture. Other seeds fell among thorns which choked out the good seed. Some seeds actually fell on good soil, yielding an abundant crop. Jesus' disciples asked him the meaning of the parable, and this is what he said:

(Verses 11-15)

> "The seed is the word of God. Those along the path are the ones who hear, and then the devil comes and takes away the word from their hearts, so that they may not believe and be saved. Those

on the rock are the ones who receive the word with joy when they hear it, but they have no root. *They believe for a while, but in the time of testing they fall away.* The seed that fell among thorns stands for those who hear, but as they go on their way they are choked by life's worries, riches and pleasures, and they do not mature. But the seed on good soil stands for those with a noble and good heart, who hear the word, retain it, and *by persevering* produce a crop."

> *Are you now abiding in Christ, persevering, overcoming?*

Can one continue the same sinful lifestyle and remain in Christ?

The answer here is very clear - *absolutely not!* When we are born again by the Spirit, we are made a "new creation" and given a new heart, one that desires to please God. The old has gone and the new has come. Love is the hallmark of this new life in Christ Jesus.

1 John 3:5-10

"But you know that he appeared so that he might take away our sins. And in him is no sin. *No one who lives in him keeps on sinning.* No one who continues to sin has either seen him or known him. Dear children, do not let anyone lead you astray. He who does what is right is righteous, just as he is righteous. He who does what is sinful is of the devil, because the devil has been sinning from the beginning. The reason the Son of God appeared was to destroy the devil's work. *No one who is born of God will continue to sin*, because God's seed remains in him; *he cannot go on sinning*, because he has been born of God. This is how we know who the children of God are and who the children of the devil are: *anyone who does not do what is right is not a child of God; nor is anyone who does not love his brother.*"

Heb. 10:26-27

"If we *deliberately keep on sinning* after we have received the knowledge of the truth, no sacrifice for sins is left, but only a fearful expectation of judgment and of raging fire that will consume the enemies of God." (Also read verses 28-31.)

(See also Ephesians 4:22-24; 1 John 3:14; 2 Corinthians 5:17 and Colossians 3:9-10)

What if I do sin?

The only sinless One is Jesus. We will always be tempted to return to our past sinful behavior, so here is the place we have a critical choice to make. It's not a sin to be tempted - the sin is in yielding to the temptation. Each time we resist makes it easier to resist the next time. Each time the temptation comes, we can turn to our advocate, who is Jesus, and ask his help.

1 John 2:1

"My dear children, I write this to you so that you will not sin. But if anybody does sin, we have one who speaks to the Father in our defense – Jesus Christ, the Righteous One."

1 Cor. 10:13

> "And God is faithful; he will not let you be tempted beyond what you can bear. But when you are tempted, he will also provide a way out so that you can stand up under it."

Many times we must take drastic steps to distance ourselves from the situations, things, or even people who pull us back into our former sinful lifestyle. You know the triggers and what influences you to do what you *know* is wrong. Don't just walk away – RUN!

1 Tim. 6:11-12

> ". . . *flee* from all this, and pursue righteousness, godliness, faith, love, endurance and gentleness. *Fight* the good fight of the faith. Take hold of the eternal life to which you were called when you made your good confession in the presence of many witnesses."

The primary root word *'châtâ'* in Hebrew that means "to miss" also means "to sin." This word is used in Judges 20:16, when seven hundred highly skilled men of the tribe of Benjamin, who were left-handed, "could sling a stone at a hair and not miss." Some translations say they never "sinned" or, in other words, they never "missed the mark." Most of us try really hard to "live" the Christian life, to be pleasing to God, to do good and be good. But most of us fall far short of always hitting the mark. We even get to the point of wanting to give up because it seems impossible to ever live a consistent Christian life. The problem may be that **WE** are trying to live a life pleasing to God in our own strength . . . and that **IS** impossible.

What man has done is to align his sights with another target – SELF. The reason man keeps missing the mark is because he is aiming at the *wrong* target. His "aim" is to please himself rather than God. The serpent's enticement to Adam and Eve was that they would become AS God. In other words, they would be little gods as wise and all-knowing as God himself. They (self) would be the center, making the rules, calling the shots, and in control instead of God. Again, that is what SIN is – I, me, myself, ruling my life. It is man declaring his independence from his Creator.

If you do fall down, get back up. First, ask God to forgive you. Next, make amends if you hurt someone with your actions, words or attitudes. Jesus gives clear instructions in Matthew 5:24 concerning the importance of reconciliation. Finally, get back on the right path. Keep your aim on pleasing God. Don't allow issues that need attention to get shoved into the "Do Later" file. Gaining and keeping a clear conscience brings a lot of joy . . . and peace. Understand that as you persevere, depending on God as your "ever-present" help, you will begin to see good changes taking place in your thinking and actions.

> *Are you missing the mark because self is dominating?*

Chapter 8

New Behaviors, New Attitudes

The moment you receive Christ into your life, you became a new person. Second Corinthians 5:17 states, "Therefore, if anyone is in Christ, he is a new creation; the old has gone, the new has come!" Something drastic has taken place. God replaced the old sinful nature with a brand new one. He takes your sins and removes them "as far as the east is from the west" (Psalms 103:12). That's a really long way! The imagery here is that God removes them far from your reach. God also says he blots out our transgressions and *remembers them no more* (Isaiah 43:25). The sin nature has been radically changed, so that you are no longer *obligated* to live as a slave to its demands. You are free to begin a completely new life that will be saturated with the Spirit of the living God himself, helping you make good choices that produce good works and good fruit. However, we don't instantly achieve sainthood, although that would be great. We have made a 180 degree turn and are embarking on a journey. I like how the Message Bible expresses this transition from old life to new:

Eph. 4:17-24

"And so I insist – and God backs me up on this – that there be no going along with the crowd, the empty-headed, mindless crowd. They've refused for so long to deal with God that they've lost touch not only with God but with reality itself. They can't think straight anymore. Feeling no pain, they let themselves go in sexual obsession, addicted to every sort of perversion. But that's no life for you. You learned Christ! My assumption is that you have paid careful attention to him, been well instructed in the truth precisely as we have it in

> Jesus. Since, then, we do not have the excuse of ignorance, everything – and I do mean everything – connected with that old way of life has to go. It's rotten through and through. Get rid of it! And then take on an entirely new way of life – a God-fashioned life, a life renewed from the inside and working itself into your conduct as God accurately reproduces his character in you."

The past is the past; it must stay in the past. The new has come; it must dominate. You will have choices to make your entire journey, which will determine what your life produces and also your eternal destiny. Just remember, you are not alone. Your best friend, Jesus, is traveling every inch of the way with you.

Is what I do important?

Absolutely! Good *works* or *deeds* are our *response* to living a life of righteousness and obedience to God. They are what we do as the visible evidence of a true follower or disciple of Jesus. In no way do they buy our salvation; good works are not a purchase, they're a response. In fact, Titus 3:8 says we are to "devote ourselves to doing what is good." Furthermore, we can expect God's help in doing good, because 2 Corinthians 9:8 says, "God is able to make all grace abound to you, so that in all things at all times, having all that you need, you will *abound in every good work*." Our works or deeds also:

Please God:

Heb. 13:16

> "And do not forget to *do good* and to share with others, for with such sacrifices God is pleased."

New Behaviors, New Attitudes

Prove repentance:

Acts 26:20

Paul declared to King Agrippa, "First to those in Damascus, then to those in Jerusalem and in all Judea, and to the Gentiles also, I preached that they should repent and turn to God and *prove their repentance by their deeds*."

Matt. 3:8

John the Baptist preached, "*Produce fruit* in keeping with repentance."

Glorify God:

Matt. 5:16

"In the same way, let your light shine before men, that they may see your *good deeds and praise your Father* in heaven."

1 Peter 2:12

"Live such good lives among the pagans that, though they accuse you of doing wrong, they may see your *good deeds and glorify God* on the day he visits us."

Store up treasure:

1 Tim. 6:18-19

"Command them to *do good*, to *be rich in good deeds*, and to be generous and willing to share. In this way they will *lay up treasure* for themselves as a firm foundation for the coming age, so that they may take hold of the life that is truly life."

New Behaviors, New Attitudes

<u>Indicate faith in action</u>:

James 2:14-26

"What good is it, my brothers, if a man claims to have faith but has no deeds? Can such faith save him? Suppose a brother or sister is without clothes and daily food. If one of you says to him, 'Go, I wish you well; keep warm and well fed,' but does nothing about his physical needs, what good is it? In the same way, faith by itself, if it is not accompanied by action, is dead. But someone will say, 'You have faith; I have deeds.' Show me your faith without deeds, and *I will show you my faith by what I do.* You believe that there is one God. Good! Even the demons believe that – and shudder. You foolish man, do you want evidence that faith without deeds is useless? Was not our ancestor Abraham considered righteous for what he did when he offered his son Isaac on the altar? You see that his faith and his actions were working together, and his faith was made complete by what he did. And the scripture was fulfilled that says, 'Abraham believed God, and it was credited to him as righteousness,' and he was called God's friend. *You see that a person is justified by what he does and not by faith alone.* In the same way, was not even Rahab the prostitute considered righteous for what she did when she gave lodging to the spies and sent them off in a different direction? *As the body without the spirit is dead, so faith without deeds is dead.*"

<u>Indicate love in action</u>:

1 John 3:16-18

"This is how we know what love is: Jesus Christ laid down his life for us. And we ought to lay down our lives for our brothers. If anyone has material possessions and sees his brother in need but has no pity on him, how can the love of God be in him? Dear children, *let us not love with words or tongue but with actions and in truth.*"

Heb. 10:24

"And let us consider how we may spur one another on toward *love and good deeds.*"

Indicate wisdom:

James 3:13

"Who is wise and understanding among you? Let him show it by his *good life*, by *deeds done* in the humility that comes from wisdom."

Are Ordained by God:

Eph. 2:10

"For we are God's workmanship, created in Christ Jesus to do good works, which God *prepared in advance for us to do.*"

Titus 2:14

"Jesus Christ gave himself for us, to redeem us from all wickedness and to purify for himself a people that are his very own, *eager to do what is good.*"

Will be tested:

1 Cor. 3:12-15

"If any man builds on this foundation using gold, silver, costly stones, wood, hay or straw, his work will be shown for what it is, because the Day will bring it to light. It will be revealed with fire, and the *fire will test the quality of each man's work*. If what he has built survives, he will receive his reward.

> If it is burned up, he will suffer loss; he himself will be saved, but only as one escaping through the flames."

<u>Will be judged</u>:

Rom. 2:6-10

> "*God will give to each person according to what he has done.* To those who by persistence in doing good seek glory, honor, and immortality, he will give eternal life. But for those who are self-seeking and who reject the truth and follow evil, there will be wrath and anger. There will be trouble and distress for every human being who does evil: first for the Jew, then for the Gentile; but glory, honor and peace for everyone who *does good*: first for the Jew, then for the Gentile."

<u>Are Known by God</u>:

> To five of the seven churches addressed in Revelation 2, 3, and 14, Jesus says, "*I know your deeds.*"

Rev. 2:23

> To the church in Thyatira he says, "I will repay each of you according to your *deeds.*"

Rev. 3:2

> To the church in Sardis he says, ". . . for I have *not found your deeds complete* in the sight of my God."

Rev. 14:13

> "Then I heard a voice from heaven say, 'Write: Blessed are the dead who die in the Lord from now on.' 'Yes,' says the Spirit, 'they will rest from their labor, for *their deeds will follow them.*'"

New Behaviors, New Attitudes

Every person who by faith accepts God's offer of salvation and becomes a true follower of Jesus **will** produce good deeds. Yes, there are many "good" people out there, who give lots of money and do really great things for others, but that alone does not make one a Christian. The verses in James chapter two explain that faith in God and works must go hand in hand. Saying you're a Christian will be backed up by what you do. Someone once asked the question, "If you were arrested for being a Christian, would there be enough evidence to convict you?" Great question! The things we do are the "evidence" to the world of who we are.

> *What kind of evidence are your deeds producing?*

Real fruit or fake?

Fruit is what God produces *in us* in response to our obedience to him and is the product of a godly life. It is proof that we are Christ's disciples. The believer has no fruitfulness apart from his union and fellowship with Christ as the true vine. In the allegory of the vine and branches in John 15, we as branches must maintain contact with the vine or we become useless and lifeless. However, verse 5 guarantees that we will bear "much fruit" if we remain in Christ. Fruit bearing is a <u>work</u> of the Holy Spirit and the <u>result</u> of our abiding *in Christ*.

John 15:1-8

> "I am the true vine, and my Father is the gardener. He cuts off every branch in me that bears no fruit, while every branch that does bear fruit he prunes

so that it will be even more fruitful. You are already clean because of the word I have spoken to you. Remain in me, and I will remain in you. No branch can bear fruit by itself; it must remain in the vine. Neither can you bear fruit unless you remain in me. I am the vine; you are the branches. If a man remains in me and I in him, he will bear much fruit; apart from me you can do nothing. If anyone does not remain in me, he is like a branch that is thrown away and withers; such branches are picked up, thrown into the fire and burned. If you remain in me and my words remain in you, ask whatever you wish, and it will be given you. This is to my Father's glory, that you bear much fruit, showing yourselves to be my disciples."

Fruit helps identify unbelievers and those who would try to deceive us with false doctrines and philosophies that would lead us away from the truth. Notice that *by their fruit* we can ascertain whether their message is truth or error. Have you ever seen a bowl of fruit that looked fresh and delicious, only to discover on close examination it was fake? We are warned in 2 Timothy 4:3-4, "For the time will come when men will not put up with sound doctrine. Instead, to suit their own desires, they will gather around them a great number of teachers to say what their itching ears what to hear. They will turn their ears away from the truth and turn aside to myths." We must carefully consider the teaching or counsel of someone before placing ourselves under their leadership. Paul tells us in Titus 1:10-11 (Message Bible): "For there are a lot of rebels out there, full of loose, confusing, and deceiving talk. Those who were brought up religious and ought to know better are the worst. . . They're disrupting entire families with their teaching, and all for the sake of a fast buck." We are not called to be judges, but wise fruit inspectors.

Matt. 7:15-20
> "Watch out for false prophets. They come to you in sheep's clothing, but inwardly they are ferocious wolves. *By their fruit you will recognize them.* Do people pick grapes from thorn bushes, or figs from thistles? Likewise, every good tree bears good fruit, but a bad tree bears bad fruit. A good tree cannot bear bad fruit, and a bad tree cannot bear good fruit. Every tree that does not bear good fruit is cut down and thrown into the fire. Thus, *by their fruit you will recognize them.*"

Ephesians 5:8-9
> "For you were once darkness, but now you are light in the Lord. Live as children of light (for the fruit of the light consists in all goodness, righteousness and truth)."

Fruit also identifies true believers, because their lives are thriving and productive. A true believer is not just *acting* like a Christian, as though he's part of the cast in some cosmic production, hanging fake fruit on the outside like a costume. His life is under the direction of the Holy Spirit, who is producing something beautiful on the inside.

Gal. 5:22-23
> "But the fruit of the Spirit is love, joy, peace, patience, kindness, goodness, faithfulness, gentleness and self-control."

Phil. 1:11
> ". . . filled with the fruit of righteousness that comes through Jesus Christ -- to the glory and praise of God."

Colossians 1:10

> "And we pray this in order that you may live a life worthy of the Lord and may *please him in every way; bearing fruit in every good work*, growing in the knowledge of God."

The very *purpose* of our union with Christ Jesus is to produce the fruit of holiness in our lives. <u>Every</u> person produces some type of fruit. Apart from Christ one produces fruit for death; joined to Christ one produces fruit for God.

Romans 7:4-5

> "So, my brothers, you also died to the law through the body of Christ, that you might belong to another, to him who was raised from the dead, in order that we might *bear fruit to God*. For when we were controlled by the sinful nature . . . we bore *fruit for death*."

James 3:17

> "But the wisdom that comes from heaven is first of all pure; then peace-loving, considerate, submissive, *full of mercy and good fruit*, impartial and sincere."

Have you examined your fruit lately?

New Behaviors, New Attitudes

Fruit-bearing happens when one spends time with Jesus. Consider the unlikely twelve Jesus selected at the very beginning of his ministry. They traveled with him witnessing the miracles, listening as he taught the crowds, asking questions, gaining understanding. Some were seasoned fishermen, another an unscrupulous tax collector, one a Zealot. We don't know the background of all these men, but we do know they struggled with doubt and fear and many of the same things with which we struggle. These common, ordinary men spent three years with Jesus learning, growing, changing, maturing, and they became the fearless leaders who brought the Gospel to the world. We, too, must become disciples.

New Behaviors, New Attitudes

Chapter 9

Becoming a Disciple or Follower

A disciple is one who is a convinced, dedicated follower of an individual or an adherent to a particular teaching or school. He also accepts and assists in spreading the doctrines of another. For a Christian, this means a convinced, dedicated follower of Jesus Christ, who helps spread the truth about Jesus, which is the gospel. In John 8:31 Jesus said, "If you hold to my teaching, you are really my disciples."

<u>What does it mean to be a disciple?</u>

Discipleship demands a commitment, a cost. Jesus was very clear on this issue. In very strong terms he admonished a large crowd in Luke 14 to estimate or count the cost of being his disciple. Jesus does not want a blind, naïve commitment that expects only blessings. He wants his followers to understand what is involved and what he expects – self-denial, a complete surrender of oneself and possessions, absolute dedication, and willing obedience. The word "daily" in Luke 9 indicates a <u>continuing action</u>, not a one-time commitment.

Luke 9:23-25

"Then he said to them all: If anyone would come after me, he must deny himself and *take up his cross daily* and follow me. For whoever wants to save his life will lose it, but whoever loses his life for me will save it. What good is it for a man to gain the whole world, and yet lose or forfeit his very self?"

Becoming a Disciple or Follower

Luke 14:26-33

> "If anyone comes to me and does not hate his father and mother, his wife and children, his brothers and sisters – yes, even his own life – he cannot be my disciple. And anyone who does not carry his cross and follow me cannot be my disciple. Suppose one of you wants to build a tower. Will he not first sit down and estimate the cost to see if he has enough money to complete it? For if he lays the foundation and is not able to finish it, everyone who sees it will ridicule him, saying, 'This fellow began to build and was not able to finish.' Or suppose a king is about to go to war against another king. Will he not first sit down and consider whether he is able with ten thousand men to oppose the one coming against him with twenty thousand? If he is not able, he will send a delegation while the other is still a long way off and will ask for terms of peace. In the same way, *any of you who does not give up everything he has cannot be my disciple.*"

Jesus had many disciples besides the twelve who formed the inner circle. They probably consisted of both men and women who had heard Jesus teach, seen his miracles, observed his actions, and were attracted to him as a person, leader, or authority figure. Even though some may have followed out of curiosity, others had probably made personal sacrifices to follow him and perhaps endured ridicule or even ostracism from family, the religious community, or both. But the proof of <u>true</u> discipleship was soon to be discovered; each had to count the cost and decide if Jesus was truly who he claimed to be. And so must we.

There is an interesting passage in John 6. Jesus had just miraculously fed the crowd of 5,000 and had gone to the opposite side of the lake. When the crowd found him the next day, they asked for a miraculous sign so they could "see it and believe him." They had just witnessed a miracle and now they wanted to see another one. Perhaps they were just wanting to be fed again. In the discussion about food that followed, Jesus declared that he is the "bread of life, the living bread that came down from heaven" (verse 48, 51). The Jews held the idea that when the Messiah came, he would do as Moses had done and send manna from heaven to feed them. Jesus corrected them as to who had sent the manna; it wasn't Moses, it was God. Now God had sent his Son as the Bread of Life, and they missed the whole point. They were offended. This wasn't what they expected. They couldn't accept that Jesus was who he said he was. After Jesus made the statements about the necessity of eating his flesh and drinking his blood, many of his disciples turned back and no longer followed him (verse 66). Those who deserted him were not ready to accept the life he offered on the terms he offered. Many seek another way, an easier way, but there is none. Either we are a disciple all the way, a follower no matter what, or we are not a disciple at all.

> *Can Jesus truly call you His disciple?*

How do I Become a Disciple and Follower of Jesus?

The way has been made; the price has been paid. There is no better time than the present. The steps are simple:

<u>Acknowledge</u> - that you understand all people are sinners, including you, and accept the fact that there is nothing you can do to pay for your own sins, earn salvation, or ever be good

enough on your own merit to deserve to live forever with a holy God.

John 3:3

> Jesus declared, "I tell you the truth, no one can see the kingdom of God unless he is born again."

Romans 3:23

> "For all have sinned and fall short of the glory of God."

<u>Believe</u> - that Jesus died to pay for your sins and was resurrected to give you eternal life. No other option exists. There is no Plan B. The gift of eternal life rests solely on what Jesus has done *for* you and will do *in* you. Jesus is the way, the bridge that brings you to God.

1 Peter 3:18

> "For Christ died for sins once for all, the righteous for the unrighteous, to bring you to God."

John 14:6

> Jesus answered, "I am the way and the truth and the life. No one comes to the Father except through me."

Acts 16:31

> "Believe on the Lord Jesus Christ, and you shall be saved."

<u>Confess</u> - your sins.

1 John 1:9

> "If we confess our sins, he is faithful and just to forgive us our sins and purify us from all unrighteousness."

Becoming a Disciple or Follower

Romans 10:9-10
> "If you confess with your mouth, 'Jesus is Lord,' and believe in your heart that God raised him from the dead, you will be saved. For it is with your heart that you believe and are justified, and it is with your mouth that you confess and are saved."

<u>Receive</u> - God's gift of His Son, Jesus. He is offering you the most awesome gift ever, better than all the treasures in the world or anything you could possibly dream of having. However, you must be willing to receive it as a gift.

John 1:12
> "Yet to all who received him, to those who believed in his name, he gave the right to become children of God."

Ephesians 2:8-9
> "For it is by grace you have been saved, through faith – and this not from yourselves, it is the gift of God – not by works, so that no one can boast."

<u>Allow</u> - the Holy Spirit full access to your life. He will guide you, teach you, and help you in every situation you face. He is the one who lives in you, produces the fruit in your life, comforts you when you hurt, and gives you everything you need to stand against sin and temptation.

Galatians 5:16
> "So I say, live by the Spirit, and you will not gratify the desires of the sinful nature."

Rom. 8:13-14
> "For if you live according to the sinful nature, you will die; but if by the Spirit you put to death the misdeeds of the body, you will live, because those who are led by the Spirit of God are sons of God."

<u>Choose daily</u> - to live for God and not for self. We are by nature self-centered, demanding our own way, choosing what will make us happy. To be quite honest, this is probably the most difficult choice we have to make – a thousand times a day. What is God's desire, not mine? Would my decision honor God? Do the words coming out of my mouth bring life or death? Does my attitude reflect the One who lives in me?

Colossians 3:3

> "For you died, and your life is now hidden with Christ in God."

2 Cor. 5:15

> "And he died for all, that those who live should no longer live for themselves but for him who died for them and was raised again."

Romans 14:8

> "If we live, we live to the Lord; and if we die, we die to the Lord. So, whether we live or die, we belong to the Lord."

Proverbs 18:21

> "The tongue has the power of life and death, and those who love it will eat its fruit."

<u>Be his witness</u> - to those in your circle of influence including family, friends, and co-workers. When people who know you see a difference, a change in you, they may ask what happened. This opens the opportunity to share your decision to be a Christ follower. The most powerful witness is your unique story. You don't need a theological degree to share what has happened in your life. As they observe changed behavior and attitudes, others will want what you have.

Becoming a Disciple or Follower

1 Peter 3:15-16
>"Always *be prepared to give an answer to everyone who asks you to give the reason for the hope that you have*. But do this with gentleness and respect, keeping a clear conscience, so that those who speak maliciously against your good behavior in Christ may be ashamed of their slander."

Colossians 4:5-6
>"Be wise in the way you act toward outsiders; make the most of every opportunity. Let your conversation be always full of grace, seasoned with salt, *so that you may know how to answer everyone*."

Just before Jesus ascended to heaven, he gave his disciples this directive: "But you will receive power when the Holy Spirit comes on you; and you will be my witnesses in Jerusalem, and in all Judea and Samaria, and to the ends of the earth" (Acts 1:8). The Holy Spirit empowers each of us to be his witnesses, too. He also gives us this warning: "If anyone is ashamed of me and my words in this adulterous and sinful generation, the Son of Man will be ashamed of him when he comes in his Father's glory with the holy angels" (Mark 8:38).

<u>Pray a prayer similar to this:</u>

According to the truth of God's Word, the Bible . . .
>I know that I am a sinner, and I understand I deserve the death penalty.
>I acknowledge there is nothing I can do to pay, earn, or deserve eternal life.
>I believe that Jesus Christ died in my place to pay the penalty for my sins.
>I am willing to turn from and forsake any and every sin in my life.
>I repent and ask you to forgive me for my sins.
>I now accept by faith the gift Jesus offers me.

I give you full access to my heart and life.
I boldly confess with my mouth that Jesus is my Lord.
I enter into a covenant with you, Father, to no longer live for myself but for you.
With your help, I will love, follow, and obey Jesus Christ.

> *"I write these things to you who believe in the name of the Son of God so that you may know that you have eternal life."*
> *1 John 5:13*

What if I begin to doubt my salvation?

Those moments will come when you need to be reminded of the commitment you have made. It helps to document the date and place of this decision for future reference. Then when the devil comes to put doubts or fears in your mind, you can say with confidence, "On the_____ day of _____at,_____, I entered into a covenant relationship with my Heavenly Father. I am His child, bought and paid for with the precious blood of His Son, Jesus Christ.

Personalize the following:

Eph. 1:13-14

> "Having believed, *I* am marked in him with a seal, the promised Holy Spirit, who is a deposit guaranteeing *my* inheritance."

Becoming a Disciple or Follower

Col. 1:13-14
> "For he has rescued *me* from the dominion of darkness and brought *me* into the kingdom of the Son he loves, in whom *I* have redemption, the forgiveness of sins."

Romans 8:16
> "The Spirit himself testifies with *my* spirit that *I* am God's child."

2 Cor. 5:21
> "God made him who had no sin to be sin for *me*, so that in him *I* might become the righteousness of God."

Rom. 8:37-39
> "In all these things *I* am more than a conqueror through him who loved *me*. For *I* am convinced that neither death nor life, neither angels nor demons, neither the present nor the future, nor any powers, neither height nor depth, nor anything else in all creation, will be able to separate *me* from the love of God that is in Christ Jesus our Lord."

"To him who is able to keep you from falling and to present you before his glorious presence without fault and with great joy – to the only God our Savior be glory, majesty, power and authority, through Jesus Christ our Lord, before all ages, now and forevermore! Amen."
Jude 1:24-25

If you just made a decision to follow Jesus Christ and to be his disciple, there is a celebration going on right now. God and the angels in heaven are dancing and singing and rejoicing over you. "The Lord your God is with you, he is mighty to save. He will take great delight in you, he will quiet you with his love, he will rejoice over you with singing" (Zephaniah 3:17). In Luke 15:7 Jesus had just told the parable of the lost sheep that was found, and then stated: "I tell you that in the same way there will be more rejoicing in heaven over one sinner who repents than over ninety-nine righteous persons who do not need to repent."

You are now launched on an incredible journey that will last a lifetime, and you don't even have to drive. You have just invited Jesus to sit in the driver's seat of your life and take you on adventures and to places of wonder. Yes, of course, there are hills and valleys and curves and bumps – sometimes even a detour. But the One who created you and loves you without reserve and beyond anything you can imagine is with you every inch of the journey. He delights in you and wants you to know Him as your best friend. As your relationship grows, his embrace becomes your place of comfort and peace, hope and joy. God's Word is the map that gives you directions and the confidence that you are on the right road. Indeed you will encounter fog and dark places and situations that you didn't expect or want, but your stability, when the storms come, is knowing that "in all things, God is working for your good" (Romans 8:28).

Along this journey, you will be learning and growing in your relationship with Jesus. You will begin to see changes taking place in your thought processes, attitudes, and desires. His wisdom will bring understanding to areas that seemed like secrets before.

A Christian never intends to go in the wrong direction, but it happens. We get sidetracked by busyness, false doctrines, materialism and many other distractions or hindrances. Like the little boy said, when asked why he kept falling out of bed, "I guess I stay too close to where I get in." That could be our problem, too. We don't get much past the "getting in" event. We must remember, however, that salvation is not just an event, it's also a process.

> *Hang on! There's more to come!*

Becoming a Disciple or Follower

CHAPTER 10

Change Points

<u>The Vine Life</u>

The greatest secret to living a Christian life is *abiding in Christ*. All our strength, all our ability to live the Christian life must come through the power of the Holy Spirit who lives in every believer. Striving to live apart from God's provision is futile. But God has given us everything we need to live an abundant and victorious Christian life.

2 Peter 1:3-4
> "His divine power has given us everything we need for life and godliness through our knowledge of him who called us by his own glory and goodness. Through these he has given us his very great and precious promises, so that through them you may participate in the divine nature and escape the corruption in the world caused by evil desires."

John 10:10
> "The thief comes only to steal and kill and destroy; I have come that they may have life, and have it *to the full.*"

John 15:7
> "If you abide in me, and my words abide in you, you will ask what you desire, and it shall be done for you." (NKJV)

What does it mean to abide? *Webster's New World Dictionary*, Second College Edition, states that to abide means "to stand fast;

remain; go on being; to stay; reside." The key to abiding in Christ is given in John 15:9-10: "As the Father has loved me, so have I loved you. Now *remain* in my love. If you <u>obey my commands</u>, you *will remain* in my love, just as I have obeyed my Father's commands and remain in his love." So what is the key? **Obedience!** Jesus carried out the Father's plan to bring mankind back into relationship with him by perfectly obeying the Father. Jesus said, "I do nothing on my own, but only what the Father has taught me" (John 8:28). Over and over Jesus emphasized that he had come to do his Father's will. As we obey, we remain in Christ. Love and obedience go hand in hand.

2 John 5b, 6

> "I ask that we *love* one another. And this is love: that we walk in *obedience* to his commands. As you have heard from the beginning, his command is that you walk in love."

On one occasion, a teacher of the law came to Jesus and asked him which of the commandments was the most important. Jesus' answer was: "Love the Lord your God with all your heart and with all your soul and with all your mind and with all your strength. The second is this: Love your neighbor as yourself. There is no commandment greater than these" (Mark 12:30-31). That's a tall order! The truth is the more we love God, the more we love others. The more we love God with our whole heart, soul, mind, and strength, the more we die to "self." However, *we* don't generate genuine love; it originates with God, who IS love. The love of God in us demands that we love one another.

1 John 4:19-21

> "We love because he first loved us. If anyone says, I love God, yet hates his brother, he is a liar. For anyone who does not love his brother, whom he has seen, cannot love God, whom he has not seen. And he has given us this command: Whoever loves God must also love his brother."

In the earlier discussion about Jesus being the true vine and we being the branches, a clear picture emerges. A branch that has been cut off from its nourishment cannot live; that branch must remain attached to the main vine in order to flourish and grow. Part of our nourishment comes from reading and studying God's Word. Reread the verses from 2 Peter quoted above. They tell us God has given us "his very great and precious promises." God is totally trustworthy. He cannot lie. He will do what he has promised. However, we need to know what those promises are. Our responsibility is to appropriate them into our lives so they can nurture us as growing Christians.

Prayer is a vital part of our nourishment. We can talk with Jesus just like we converse with our best friend. The hard part is learning to listen. Jesus plainly tells us in John 10:27-28: "My sheep *listen* to my voice; I know them, and they follow me. I give them eternal life, and they shall never perish; no one can snatch them out of my hand." Our part is to listen and follow. His part is to know us, protect us, and give us eternal life. A great exchange, don't you think? Throughout my life, some of my greatest joys have been hearing the voices of those I love. I know my husband's voice well and recognize it in a crowd of people. I loved hearing our young sons laughing and talking together as they played. They are grown men now, but I still recognize their voices anywhere. So, too, we learn to recognize the voice of Jesus as we listen. Seldom do I hear an audible voice, but he often speaks deep in my heart and mind with such clarity that I know who it is. Sometimes I sense his speaking to me as I read the Bible or while listening to a sermon; sometimes another person will say something that resonates inside my spirit. Listening must be practiced, but you will come to *know* his voice.

Forgive Those Offenders!

Unforgiveness is one of the greatest detriments to living a life pleasing to God. We nurse grudges and hang onto offenses because we feel justified in doing so. What we don't realize is that holding grudges and harboring resentment is like a chain or massive cord that binds us to that person, allowing them to control our thoughts and feelings, and sometimes even our actions. We think about them, the incident, or injustice against us continually; the problem keeps circling around and around in our heads. We desire revenge and think about doing the same thing to them (or worse) so they will know how it feels to be treated like they treated us. We want justice and consider taking matters into our own hands to bring that about. We become the arresting officer, the prosecuting attorney, the jury, the judge, and the jailer. Those evildoers are indeed guilty and they *will* pay! The problem is, however, that we have convicted them and placed them in a prison of our own making, not realizing that we are the one locked up. We are kept captive in our mind and imagination every time we see them or think of them. This obsession is killing us and keeping us from moving forward, but somehow, we feel justified. It's like drinking poison and expecting the other person to die. God always gives us the choice: *handle things ourselves or allow Him to handle them*. Letting go of the offense releases the offender so God can deal with him. Our plans often don't have the end result we desired, but God's plans never fail.

Probably the saddest thing I have ever heard someone say is, "I will *never* forgive that person for what he/she did!" The Bible tells us there are serious consequences in <u>not</u> forgiving someone. Consider what Jesus said:

Matt. 6:14-15

> "For if you forgive men when they sin against you, your heavenly Father will also forgive you. But *if you do not forgive* men their sins, your Father *will not forgive your sins.*"

That's serious! Our decision to not forgive others brings tragic consequences for us. God will not forgive us! We may not feel like forgiving someone, but forgiveness is not an act of our feelings, it's an act of our will. We *will* forgive or we *won't* forgive. When we *will* to forgive, we don't usually get warm, fuzzy feelings for that person. What does happen is that the intense need for revenge is gone. A sense of freedom takes its place. Forgiveness is the key that unlocks the door of our self-made prison and releases both that person and us. We give him to God, the Just Judge of the Universe, to deal with in his time and way. (Romans 12:19) We are free! We don't have to worry about that offender, the results of his actions, or the punishment for his sins. He is totally in God's hands and God will take care of everything. Just don't try to tell God how to handle his business; let God be God. When bad thoughts or feelings try to creep back in, we remind ourselves that we have given the person and circumstances to God, and he is now in charge, not us and not the offender. By forgiving that person, you give up your right to remain angry or hold onto grudges.

Colossians 3:13
> "Bear with each other and forgive whatever grievances you may have against one another. Forgive as the Lord forgave you."

Ephesians 4:32
> "Be kind and compassionate to one another, forgiving each other, just as in Christ God forgave you."

Who do you have locked up?

Gain a Clear Conscience

Bill Gothard, founder of the Institute in Basic Youth Conflicts, stated in one of his seminar resources titled *Research in Principles of Life*: "A clear conscience involves that inner freedom of spirit toward God and others that comes by knowing that God's holiness is not offended by one's thought or action, and that no one can point a finger at you and say, 'You've offended me, and you've never asked for my forgiveness.'" Our first response when we recognize we have had an offensive response or sinful behavior, whether in word, thought or deed, is to ask God to forgive us. Isaiah 59:2 tells us: "But your iniquities have separated you from your God; your sins have hidden his face from you, so that he will not hear." Sin drives a wedge between us and God if we allow it to remain in our hearts and lives. A Holy God will not cohabit with sin. Hebrews 12:1 instructs us ". . . to *throw off everything that hinders and the sin that so easily entangles*, and let us run with perseverance the race marked out for us." Learn to keep a clear conscience between you and God.

One of the most wonderful, freeing, satisfying activities, as you begin to grow as a Christian, is to identify and deal with past wrongs you have committed or in which you were an active participant. Not only must you forgive the person who offended or wronged you, you must take *decisive action* to seek forgiveness of those whom you offended or wronged. Begin to make a list as you find yourself thinking about certain events or situations that still trouble you. Maybe the incident seemed insignificant to you at the time, but if the memory keeps returning and you never made it right, you probably need to deal with it. Perhaps restitution needs to be made or your relationship with that person needs to be restored. Put it on the list.

Gaining a clear conscience requires humility on our part, which is not an easy task for most of us. Our pride will try to hold us back, making excuses or convincing us to not seek forgiveness from someone. Pride tells us *they* were wrong, too, the incident wasn't that big a deal, the timing isn't right, and the list goes on. If we allow pride to block seeking forgiveness from others, we will never gain a clear conscience.

Proverbs 16:18
> "Pride goes before destruction, a haughty spirit before a fall."

Proverbs 8:13
> God says, "I hate pride and arrogance, evil behavior and perverse speech."

Why is pride so adamant? Why does God hate pride? Because pride is **sin** and must not continue to rule us. Pride revolves around ourselves and is always self-seeking. Allowing pride to sit on the throne of our hearts instead of God is more than serious; it's dangerous. It breaks relationship with God. We have rejected God as God in our lives and replaced it with self. Dethroning pride is dealing a death blow to prideful *self* and allowing God to take his rightful place. As we consciously humble ourselves before the Lord, he will give us everything we need to kick pride out the door. When we accepted God's gift of salvation, he redeemed or freed us from the *power* of sin. Sin can no longer rule over us. . . unless we allow it to.

Romans 6:14
> "For sin shall not be your master. . ."

Micah 6:8
> "He has showed you, O man, what is good. And what does the Lord require of you? To act justly and to love mercy and to *walk humbly with your God.*"

It takes humility to admit our part in wrongdoing. It takes humility to seek out someone we have hurt and say, "Will you forgive me?" Asking forgiveness *will* humble us and making that choice will bring self and pride under the rule of Jesus Christ.

God will lift us up and give us the grace to do what we need to do. The Holy Spirit will help us both identify and deal with sin and past offenses, so we can gain a clear conscience.

James 4:10

> "Humble yourselves before the Lord, and *he will lift you up.*"

Proverbs 3:34

> "God opposes the proud but *gives grace to the humble.*"

When making a sincere apology, it's important not to be flippant or have a wrong attitude. I grew up with two sisters and we had our differences. Our parents taught us to apologize when we were unkind to each other, so we would grudgingly say, "I'm sorry!" Usually my apology was not done in a spirit of love, but out of obligation. Because our offenses were frequent, we started using a shorter version of an apology by saying, "S." We never named our offense and none of our apologies evoked a response. Little did I know there is a right way and a wrong way to ask for forgiveness. The wrong way usually includes a disclaimer, such as: "I apologize *if* I offended you," or "I guess I was wrong, so I'm sorry," or "I'm really sorry, but it wasn't all my fault." Other ways which don't work are simply saying, "I'm sorry" or "I apologize." A genuine act of forgiveness *names the offense* and *evokes a response.* Try this:

> I remember when I_____ (name offense) and realize how wrong that was. I know I hurt you and I've come to ask for your forgiveness. Will you forgive me?
>
> Or if the offense was very recent, you could simply say: "Will you forgive me for_____ (name offense). That was unkind of me (or whatever word is appropriate).

If there is a time lapse since the offense, before calling or visiting the offended person, write out your apology. Include the specific offense and say, "Will you forgive me?" If restitution is involved, be prepared to pay back or return whatever was taken. They may or may not choose to forgive you. If they refuse to forgive, it's now between them and God. They may hesitate simply because they want to see if your apology is sincere as evidenced by your life. They may never plan to forgive you, but would rather feel justified in holding a grudge. Remember, you have done your part and can have a clear conscience, with or without their acceptance. Don't allow yourself to be pulled into an argument over the situation. There are always two sides to a story, and you didn't come to rehearse everything. You came to take care of your part of the offense, not justify or blame. Be brief, sincere, and genuinely humble. After you feel you have gained a clear conscience with everyone you have violated or offended, learn to keep short accounts with both God and others. What glorious freedom you will experience!

A word of caution: calling or visiting the person is the best choice. Writing in any form cannot adequately convey your heart, which is an important part of a truly sincere, humble apology. Also, you may not want to have a written record of the offense for which you are asking forgiveness.

> *Have you asked forgiveness and cleared your conscience?*

Examining Motives and Attitudes

Earlier we looked at the story in Luke 8:5-15, about the farmer who sowed seed and the results depending on where the seed fell. Jesus explained, "The seed is the word of God. Those along the path are the ones who hear, and then the devil comes and takes away the word from their hearts, so that they may not believe and be saved. Those on the rock are the ones who receive the word with joy when they hear it, but they have no root. They believe for a while, but in the time of testing they fall away. The seed that fell among thorns stands for those who hear, but as they go on their way they are choked by life's worries, riches and pleasures, and they do not mature. But the seed on good soil stands for those with a noble and good heart, who hear the word, retain it, and by persevering produce a crop." (Verses 11-15) The particular aspect to examine here is the soil quality.

Notice that where the seed fell was either hard-packed and trampled, rocky, or weed infested. The seed that produced a good crop had good soil. How can we achieve this good, fertile soil? How can we allow God's word to impact our lives with fruitfulness? The key is in understanding the three levels on which all of us operate.

The Overt Level: Overt means "open to view." This is the level of visible behavior or what we do that others can see. Sin in this area consists of activities like adultery, theft, murder, excessive living, cheating, gossip, etc. Good deeds on this level include giving aid, serving others, tithing, being a good employee, witnessing, encouraging, working in the church, volunteering, etc. For the most part, this is where the world lives and places its emphasis. Many Christians never get any deeper than this. They think if they STOP smoking, drinking, cussing and running around and START praying, witnessing, going to church and reading the Bible, they will be living a Christian life. You would have to agree that improvement has been made. Right?

The Covert Level: Covert means "covered over, concealed, sheltered, secret, or veiled." This is the level of thoughts and emotions known only to ourselves. Sin here includes lust, greed, hatred, envy, jealousy, pride, covetousness, or the thoughts and emotions behind overt sin. Good deeds on this level are faithfulness, humility, love, generosity, or things which cannot be seen except for the actions they cause. This area is where most *serious* believers end up. They understand that obedience to the Lord includes their very thoughts and feelings, not just outward actions. This level is considered the "bottom line" of Christian living. If we have brought every thought and emotion into obedience to Christ (see 2 Corinthians 10:5), then we've mastered Christian discipline and maturity. We've ARRIVED!

The Basement Level: The third level is the REAL you, the very basement of your soul. The majority of Christians are not even aware it exists, but it is the strongest factor in determining the direction of a person's life. Proverbs 4:23 tells us, "Above all else, guard your heart, for it is the wellspring of life." In reference to a body of water, a spring is the source or origin of that body of water. Springs of life are the origin of our soul, the source of the "real me." This is the area of our ***motives and attitudes***. Springs of water are generally hidden, but you can see everything that flows out of them. The same is true of our motives and attitudes. We rarely see or define them, but what flows out of them governs everything that is in the rest of our lives. Matthew 12:34 says, "For out of the overflow of the heart the mouth speaks." Problems in our motives and attitudes that are never recognized and never dealt with can grow into major areas of deception and destruction.

Jesus defined these three areas in the Sermon on the Mount, found in Matthew, chapters 5-7. The people he was speaking to were raised primarily with emphasis on "overt" living – DOING religious things: (a) keep the Law of Moses, (b) conform to the accepted standard of right, and (c) you will be in good standing with God.

Jesus shows them that there is more to the Kingdom of God than what we DO. Little by little he is making them aware of the *real* demands of the Kingdom of God.

> Matt. 5:21 & 22 says, "Do not murder . . ." (Overt). "But I tell you that anyone who is angry with his brother will be subject to judgment" (Covert).

> Verses 27 & 28 says, "Do not commit adultery . . ." (Overt). But I tell you that anyone who looks at a woman lustfully has already committed adultery . . ." (Covert).

> Matt. 6:1 says, "Be careful not to do your 'acts of righteousness' before men, to be seen by them" (Overt). "But when you give to the needy, do not let your left hand know what your right hand is doing, so that your giving may be in secret" (Covert).

Jesus is touching on the *motive* behind much of the religious activity of his day. On the outside, the religious leaders acted holy and righteous and kept the law, but at the source, their motives were impure. They desired to be seen or noticed, not only in their giving, but also when they prayed (Matt. 6:5) and fasted (Matt. 6:16). Any activity, no matter how good, is condemned as hypocrisy if it is done from a wrong motive. So what is a motive?

A motive is why I *act* the way I do. Motives are the things which motivate me to action or non-action. The word motive is derived from the word "motor," which are devices that make us go. For example: My motive for getting out of bed and going to work every day is to earn money so I can pay my bills. Or maybe my motive for attending church is because my reputation would be tarnished if I didn't go.

An attitude is why I *react* the way I do. Attitudes are a person's feelings, posture, or understanding of a given issue or situation. For example: "I feel cheated;" "the government owes me a living;" "it makes me angry every time I get cut off in traffic." Attitudes are my perspective on life, my measuring stick to size up and interpret every situation. They are the "glasses" through which I see life. The color of my attitudes determines the color I see in every experience and situation.

Most of people's emotional and behavioral hang-ups come from a root problem in the motives and attitudes. Without changing our motives and attitudes, behavior cannot become truly holy. It's usually just suppressed or modified to some other form. "Polluted" springs will never produce clear water. James 3:10-12 states it well. "Out of the same mouth come praise and cursing. My brothers, this should not be. Can both fresh water and salt water flow from the same spring? My brothers, can a fig tree bear olives, or a grapevine bear figs? Neither can a salt spring produce fresh water." In the same way, no matter how much we pray, fast, and discipline ourselves, if our motives and attitudes are impure, our behavior will never significantly change. The soil that produces true fruitfulness can only be achieved as we allow the Holy Spirit access to the "basement." Jesus stated it clearly in Matthew 7:16-18, "By their fruit you will recognize them. Do people pick grapes from thorn bushes, or figs from thistles? Likewise, every good tree bears good fruit, but a bad tree bears bad fruit. A good tree cannot bear bad fruit, and a bad tree cannot bear good fruit."

So, what is the right motivation? We can find that in Matthew 6:33, "Seek first the kingdom of God and his righteousness." Ask yourself, "Is my motivation self-seeking?" "Am I doing this to glorify me or God?" "Was that reaction or feeling pleasing to the Lord or offensive?"

> *What motivates you?*
> *Do your responses betray you?*

Expose Those Blind Spots

All of us have hidden areas, also called "blind spots," which hinder our growth as a Christian and cause others to be offended. We can readily see the faults of others, but are "blind" to our own imperfections, which may have become habits. We may be excusing many of these offensive ways by saying, "That's just the way I am." However, that's not the way you have to remain. Maybe you have never thought of some of your actions, motives, or attitudes as being wrong, but asking God to show us our heart is where change starts.

Psalm 139:23-24
> "Search me, O God, and know my heart; test me and know my anxious thoughts. See if there is any offensive way in me, and lead me in the way everlasting."

Search me, know me, look and see what's inside that are blind spots to me. This prayer is the MRI of our heart, the **M**any **R**evealing **I**nsights that God will begin to show us that he desires to change. Jeremiah 17:9-10 tells us, "The heart is deceitful above all things and beyond cure. Who can understand it? I the Lord search the heart and examine the mind." Only God can reveal the motives, the attitudes, the wrong thinking, the unbelief, the pride, the hypocrisy. Only the Holy Spirit can show us the sin that lurks in the deepest recesses of our hearts, those things that are offensive, hinder our growth and destroy our testimony. Our car has a safety feature that flashes a yellow light on the outside mirror when you activate your turn signal and a car is in your blind spot. A dangerous situation can be avoided if we pay attention to the flashing safety light. In much the same way, the Holy Spirit flashes his light into our hearts to warn us of the dangers lurking in the blind spots of our lives. The good news is that God will steer us clear of those dangers and effect changes in us as we allow him access and opportunity. Don't ignore the warning signals.

Heb. 12:14-15
> "Make every effort to live in peace with all men and to be holy; without holiness no one will see the Lord. See to it that no one misses the grace of God and that no bitter root grows up to cause trouble and defile many."

Matthew 7:3-5
> "Why do you look at the speck of sawdust in your brother's eye and pay no attention to the plank in your own eye? How can you say to your brother, 'Let me take the speck out of your eye,' when all the time there is a plank in your own eye? You hypocrite, first take the plank out of your own eye, and then you will see clearly to remove the speck from your brother's eye."

Seeing the faults and shortcomings of others is easy; taking an honest look at ourselves is difficult. We humans all grew up in a less than perfect world, and most of us in a less than perfect environment, which critically impacted our thinking, actions and emotions. Many of our undesirable issues most likely can be traced to seeds planted when we were very young and then allowed to remain and be nurtured into adulthood. Examples set forth by those we trusted or looked up to, both good and bad, also made a tremendous impact on us. As we mature, we begin to view life through lenses tinted (or tainted) by a blend of our experiences, personality, and perceptions. We tend to get a distorted view of ourselves, others, and life in general. What we have accepted as "normal" may not be healthy, but a hindrance to seeing the truth about ourselves. The faults in others that irritate us the most are usually some of our faults, too. We may have excused it in ourselves, but are quick to criticize it in others. Allowing the Holy Spirit to turn a spotlight on our hearts will reveal many of those "planks" or blind spots that will obstruct our view of truth.

The Bible is clear that "God our Savior wants all men to be saved and to come to a knowledge of the truth" (1 Timothy 2:3-4). We must be willing to accept the truth as set forth in the Bible, not what society endorses as acceptable.

John 8:31-32

> "If you hold to my teaching, you are really my disciples. Then *you will know the truth, and the truth will set you free.*"

John 14:6

> "Jesus answered, 'I am the way and *the truth* and the life. No one comes to the Father except through me."

The reason we ask the Holy Spirit to do an MRI on our hearts is because he is the *Spirit of truth*. In John 14:16-17, Jesus told his disciples, "I will ask the Father, and he will give you another Counselor to be with you forever – the *Spirit of truth*. The world cannot accept him, because it neither sees him nor knows him. But you know him, for he lives with you and will be in you." As a child of God, you have the Holy Spirit living within you, and he will lead you to the truth.

John 16:13

> But when he, the Spirit of truth, comes, *he will guide you into all truth.*"

We don't need to be afraid to allow the Holy Spirit to search our hearts with his spotlight and expose the darkness that tries to hide there. He is tender and loving and knows everything about us. Our response as we become aware of our blind spots, which include attitudes as well as actions, is to say, "Yes, I release this area to you now. Thank you for your revealing work in my heart and life to change and mature me." You can rest assured the changes will bring great freedom.

Have you scheduled your MRI?

Change Points

Chapter 11

Encountering Adversity

After you become a Christian, regardless of what you may have heard from good intentioned, albeit, misinformed people, life does not become an instant utopia or a lifetime vacation on the beach free from all problems. Trials are a part of life. Nor will we necessarily *know* what the trial is about or exactly what God is working out, but we can know it's "not for nothing." God is working *good* – his good purpose for our good. At times God may give you understanding or impress upon you the purpose while you are in the middle of crisis. At other times, long after the trail is over, you will look back and see where your thinking changed, a relationship was deepened, or wisdom was gained. Other times you may remain clueless. It's those in-between times, those times of not understanding, that challenge our faith.

When Jesus was talking with his disciples, preparing them for what was about to happen to him, he told them he was going away but would send the Holy Spirit to them. He let them know they wouldn't see him for a little while, but then they would see him again for a little while (John 16:16). He was speaking of his death and resurrection, but it was hard for the disciples to understand. They were confused and filled with grief, so he said, "I have told you these things, so that *in me* you may have peace. In this world *you will have trouble*. But take heart! I have overcome the world" (John 16:33). The bad news is, we *will* have problems and trouble because we live in a fallen world. The good news is, Jesus has overcome the world, and *in him* we can have peace . . . in spite of our circumstances. We are also told there is a reason for the problems that come into our lives.

James 1:2-4

> "Consider it *pure joy*, my brothers, whenever you face trials of many kinds, because *you know* that the testing of your faith develops perseverance. Perseverance must finish its work so that you may be mature and complete, not lacking anything."

The words *joy* and *trial* in this verse don't seem to go together; they're like an oxymoron. And not just joy, *pure* joy. Are you kidding me? These two words shouldn't be used in the same sentence. How can we consider it pure joy when we face trials? That doesn't even sound possible.

The answer lies in the next statement: "because you know." How much easier are the trials when we understand there is a reason and a purpose behind what is happening. Trials are meant to produce perseverance in us – determination, grit, tenacity, resolve, the ability to hang in there, the stamina to finish the race. The end result is our maturity. God is making us complete. Verse 12 says, "Blessed is the man (or woman) who perseveres under trial, because when he has stood the test, he will receive the crown of life that God has promised to those who love him." What a reward! We can't give up. We've got to keep going in spite of the challenges.

Galatians 5:7

> "You were running a good race. Who cut in on you and kept you from obeying the truth?"

The Apostle Paul would have related well to our world of sports and super athletes. He often spoke of the Christian life as running a race and "pressing on toward the goal to win the prize" (Philippians 3:12-14). In this race, however, we are participants by our own choosing; no one forced us to sign up. This is individual, not team competition; we cannot tag in and out or expect someone else to carry the baton for us. We are solely responsible for finishing this race. This is not to say we are left to struggle on our own. Absolutely not! We are part of the Body of Christ, a community of believers, who will run alongside us, cheering, encouraging, teaching, loving and helping us. However, they are not ultimately responsible for our choices; we are. To continue to run the race and not drop out, even in the face of opposition and trials, is wholly up to each individual. So Paul asks a piercing question: "Who cut in on you and kept you from obeying the truth?" Indeed, who can we blame for not following Christ? Who *made* us disobey? Who is responsible for our not walking in *truth*? Who made us quit before the finish line? Great questions!

> *Who are you blaming, or what is keeping you from obeying the truth?*

Suffering

Another term used interchangeably with trials and problems and bad stuff happening to us is "suffering." We may suffer with sickness, disease, accident, injury, loss of a loved one or a relationship, loss of a job or a home, financial distress, or any number of things. Suffering is real and all of us face stressful situations, many times to the point that it affects our body, mind, and emotions. We often become discouraged and can spiral into depression. We wonder where God is in all this and if he even cares. Peter, one of Jesus' disciples - the feisty one - addressed this problem area:

1 Peter 4:19 & 5:10

> "Those who suffer according to God's will should commit themselves to their faithful Creator and continue to do good. And the God of all grace, who called you to his eternal glory in Christ, after you have suffered a little while, will himself restore you and make you strong, firm and steadfast."

There are only two avenues of suffering: that which we bring on ourselves as a result of walking in rebellion to God, and that which God allows in our lives as his children. And herein lies the problem with our <u>response</u> to suffering. If we do not *wholly* trust God, if we are suspicious of his motives, if we question his love, if we think he may be mad at us for some unknown reason, or if we feel we can't ever please him, then we *will not* and *cannot* respond in faith. We see suffering as punishment. But if we are walking as an obedient child of God, then God is always working for our good (Romans 8:28). We are suffering "according to his will," and we are to commit ourselves to his faithful work in us. What's hard is when the situation isn't remedied within a limited time frame. The trial continues on and on, sometimes for months or years, and we grow weary. Will this never end? Will the answer never come? We are instructed to *commit* and *continue*: <u>commit</u> to God's faithful work in us and <u>continue</u> to do good.

Galatians 6:9

> "Let us not become weary in doing good, for at the proper time we will reap a harvest *if we do not give up*."

When we "do good" we are moving outside our own little world and present crisis, and focusing on others. Something supernatural happens and we find healing taking place; grief is being replaced with peace and even joy. And in "a little while" God himself will "restore you and make you strong, firm and steadfast." Rejoice! This is only for a season, *a little while*, and won't last forever.

Discipline

If you are a parent, you know that discipline is a critical part of rearing obedient, respectful children. Left to themselves, children will be self-centered, disrespectful, rebellious, spoiled brats. With no boundaries or guidelines they will choose what makes them happy, not what is best for them. You discipline them because you love them and want them to grow into responsible adults, capable of navigating life well by making wise choices. Applying discipline isn't always a pleasant experience for the child. Neither is God's discipline in the lives of his children.

Hebrews 12:5-11

> "My son, do not make light of the Lord's discipline, and do not lose heart when he rebukes you, because the Lord disciplines those he loves, and he punishes everyone he accepts as a son. Endure hardship as discipline; God is treating you as sons. For what son is not disciplined by his father? If you are not disciplined (and everyone undergoes discipline), then you are illegitimate children and not true sons. Moreover, we have all had human fathers who disciplined us and we respected them for it. How much more should we submit to the Father of our spirits and live! Our fathers disciplined us for a little while as they thought best; but God disciplines us for our good, that we may share in his holiness. No discipline seems pleasant at the time, but painful. Later on, however, it produces a harvest of righteousness and peace for those who have been trained by it."

We need a willing heart to receive the rebukes and corrections of the Lord, because he is bringing positive changes that will affect our spiritual development. God expects us to grow up and mature in our faith, so he is working to correct our faults, adjust our attitudes, and help us gain wisdom. What is wisdom?

It's seeing life from God's point of view so we can understand the relationship between our problems and God's principles. Proverbs 9:10 states, "The fear of the Lord is the beginning of wisdom, and knowledge of the Holy One is understanding." Wisdom enables us to respond to life's situations in a way that honors God. Those who refuse to learn and embrace God's gift of wisdom are "always learning but never able to acknowledge the truth" (2 Timothy 3:7). God calls them fools. One can have an impressive collection of Ph.D's, but devoid of God's wisdom, he has only information, which can lead to pride. On the flip side, we have only to ask and receive God's wisdom by faith.

James 1:5-6
> "If any of you lacks wisdom, he should ask God, who gives generously to all without finding fault, and it will be given to him. But when he asks, he must believe and not doubt . . ."

Proverbs 5:21-23
> "For a man's ways are in full view of the Lord, and he examines all his paths. The evil deeds of a wicked man ensnare him; the cords of his sin hold him fast. *He will die for lack of discipline*, led astray by his own great folly."

Proverbs 12:1
> "Whoever loves discipline loves knowledge, but he who hates correction is stupid."

Okay. So as a Christian am I supposed to be *happy* about adversity? Do I just paste a smile on my face and declare, "I'm just fine, thank you," when inside I'm drowning in pain? Let's look at Jesus' response in Hebrews 12:2: "Who for the *joy* set before him endured the cross, scorning its shame, and sat down at the right hand of the throne of God." Was Jesus *happy* about having to go to the cross? I think not. Just before the end, he was in agony, crying out to his Father to spare him this "cup" if possible (Luke 22:41-44). Notice he *endured* the cross and *scorned* its shame. He did what he had to do; he endured. The "joy set before him" was in knowing he was doing the will of the Father. There was a plan and a purpose for the cross. Jesus' joy was in knowing he was accomplishing eternal redemption for mankind. The *Message Bible* says, "He never lost sight of where he was headed." He stayed focused, looking beyond the trial to the purpose, knowing that his perseverance and faithfulness would bring its reward.

In the same way, we *endure* trials and hardship, knowing there is something greater at work in our lives. Sometimes we cry, we hurt, we might even get mad at God for a season simply because we don't understand what's going on. The Bible gives us numerous examples of people who endured very painful trials and their responses to the trials. Elijah ran; Abraham lied; Moses got angry; Jacob wrestled; Jesus sweat blood. We will not be devoid of emotion, we are human. But at some point, we will be able to *scorn*, or literally *laugh at*, our present troubles because we know God is working His divine purposes in us.

We are reminded in 1 Peter 4:12-16: "Dear friends, do not be surprised at the painful trial you are suffering, as though something strange were happening to you. But rejoice that you participate in the sufferings of Christ, so that you may be overjoyed when his glory is revealed. If you are insulted because of the name of Christ, you are blessed, for the Spirit of glory and of God rests on you. If you suffer, it should not be as a murderer or thief or any other kind of criminal, or even as a meddler. However, if you suffer as a Christian, do not be ashamed, but praise God that you bear that name." Getting a correct perspective on the difficulties we are going through helps keep us tethered to the One who is leading the way through our darkness. His grip is secure, and when we are too weary to walk another step, he carries us.

2 Cor. 4:17-18

"For our light and momentary troubles are achieving for us an eternal glory that far outweighs them all. So we fix our eyes not on what is seen, but on what is unseen. For what is seen is temporary, but what is unseen is eternal."

> *Are you allowing God's wisdom to help you see life's challenges from His perspective?*

Chapter 12

God's Provisions – Our Heritage

Although God's love extends to all mankind, he has made available wonderful provisions to those who have accepted his gift of eternal life through Jesus Christ and are living in covenant relationship with him. The Psalmist tells us, "All the ways of the Lord are loving and faithful for those who keep the demands of his covenant" (Psalm 25:10). Below are listed only a few of the vast number of promises, which are part of your heritage as a true Christian. We are told that "no matter how many promises God has made, they are 'Yes' in Christ" (2 Corinthians 1:20). As you read and study the Bible, you will find treasures, insights, and wisdom beyond anything you can imagine. Most importantly, however, you will find **truth**, which can only be found in Jesus Christ.

<u>God's love is great and eternal</u>. God IS love!

1 John 3:1

> "How *great is the love the Father has lavished on us*, that we should be called children of God! And that is what we are! The reason the world does not know us is that it did not know him."

John 3:16

> "For *God so loved the world* that he gave his one and only Son, that whoever believes in him shall not perish but have eternal life."

Romans 5:8

> "But *God demonstrates his own love for us* in this: While we were still sinners, Christ died for us."

Psalm 117:2
> "For *great is his love toward us*, and the faithfulness of the Lord endures forever."

(See also Ephesians 2:4-7; 1 John 4:9-12, 19; Psalm 107:43; Psalm 118:1)

<u>God is faithful and just</u>; we can count on that.

1 Cor. 1:8-9
> "He will keep you strong to the end, so that you will be blameless on the day of our Lord Jesus Christ. *God*, who has called you into fellowship with his Son Jesus Christ our Lord, *is faithful*."

Psalm 33:4
> "For the word of the Lord is right and true; *he is faithful in all he does*."

1 John 1:9
> "If we confess our sins, *he is faithful and just* and will forgive us our sins and purify us from all unrighteousness."

2 Thessalonians 3:3
> "But the *Lord is faithful*, and he will strengthen and protect you from the evil one."

(See also 1 Thessalonians 5:24; 2 Thessalonians 1:6-7; 2 Timothy 2:13; Psalm 146:5-6; Revelation 19:11)

<u>God will always be with us and help us</u> through those times of trial, testing, suffering and persecution. We are not promised a life of ease, but we are promised that He will be "ever-present."

Matthew 28:20
> "And surely *I am with you always*, to the very end of the age."

Hebrews 13:5-6
> "God has said, '*Never will I leave you; never will I forsake you.*' So we say with confidence, 'The Lord is my helper; I will not be afraid; What can man do to me?'"

2 Peter 2:9
> "The Lord knows how to *rescue godly men from trials* and to hold the unrighteous for the day of judgment."

(See also Psalm 37: 32-33; Revelation 3:10; Psalm 91:15 and 1 Corinthians 10:13)

<u>God is our provider</u> to meet our needs, not necessarily to check off everything on our "got-to-have-it" list.

Philippians 4:19
> "And my God will meet *all your needs* according to his glorious riches in Christ Jesus."

Psalm 23:1
> "The Lord is my shepherd; *I shall not be in want.*"

2 Corinthians 9:6, 8
> "Whoever sows sparingly will also reap sparingly, and whoever sows generously will also reap generously. And God is able to make all grace abound to you, so that in all things at all times, *having all that you need*, you will abound in every good work."

Psalm 34:9-10

> "Fear the Lord, you his saints, for those who fear him *lack nothing*. The lions may grow weak and hungry, but those who seek the Lord *lack no good thing*."

(See also 2 Corinthians 9:10; Psalm 84:11; Luke 6:38; Psalm 107:8-9)

<u>He has given us angels</u> to watch over us and minister to us.

Hebrews 1:14

> "Are not all angels ministering spirits sent to serve those who will inherit salvation?"

Psalm 91:9-11

> "If you make the Most High your dwelling–even the Lord, who is my refuge–then no harm will befall you, no disaster will come near your tent. For he will command his angels concerning you to guard you in all your ways."

Psalm 34:7

> "The angel of the Lord encamps around those who fear him, and he delivers them."

(See also Acts 12:7-11; Matthew 18:10; Hebrews 13:2; Luke 1:26-28)

<u>God is our protector</u> and rescues us.

Psalm 91:14

> "Because he loves me, says the Lord, I will rescue him; I will protect him, for he acknowledges my name."

Psalm 32:7
> "You are my hiding place; you will protect me from trouble and surround me with songs of deliverance."

John 17:11
> Jesus prayed, "Holy Father, protect them by the power of your name."

2 Thessalonians 3:3
> "But the Lord is faithful, and he will strengthen and protect you from the evil one."

(See also Proverbs 2:7, 8 & 11; Psalm 37:28; Psalm 5:11-12; John 17:12-15; 2 Timothy 4:18; Proverbs 3:21-26)

<u>God will guide us</u> as we navigate life and seek truth.

John 16:13
> "But when he, the Spirit of truth, comes, he will guide you into all truth."

Psalm 23:3
> "He restores my soul, he guides me in paths of righteousness for his name's sake."

Isaiah 48:17
> "This is what the Lord says – your Redeemer, the Holy One of Israel: I am the Lord your God, who teaches you what is best for you, who directs you in the way you should go."

Proverbs 20:24a
> "A man's steps are directed by the Lord."

(See also Psalm 119:35, 133; Psalm 73:24; Psalm 37:23; Isaiah 58:11; Psalm 25:9; Proverbs 3:6; Proverbs 16:9)

<u>He gives us courage</u>, strength and confidence to do what he has called us to do.

Philippians 4:13
> "I can do everything through him who gives me strength."

2 Corinthians 12:9
> "My grace is sufficient for you, for my power is made perfect in weakness."

Colossians 1:11
> ". . . being strengthened with all power according to his glorious might so that you may have great endurance and patience . . ."

Ephesians 6:10
> "Finally, be strong in the Lord and in his mighty power."

Psalm 18:32
> "It is God who arms me with strength and makes my way perfect."

(See also Ephesians 3:16-21; Mark 6:49-50; Acts 4:13; 1 Peter 5:10; 2 Thessalonians 2:16-17; 2 Timothy 1:7; Proverbs 3:26)

<u>He provides healing, deliverance and health</u>

Matthew 8:16
> "When evening came, many who were demon-possessed were brought to him, and he drove out the spirits with a word and healed all the sick."

Proverbs 4:20-22
> "My son, pay attention to what I say; listen closely to my words. Do not let them out of your sight,

keep them within your heart; for they are life to those who find them and *health to a man's whole body.*"

Jeremiah 30:17
"I will restore you to health and heal your wounds, declares the Lord."

James 5:14-15
"Is any one of you sick? He should call the elders of the church to pray over him and anoint him with oil in the name of the Lord. And the prayer offered in faith will make the sick person well; the Lord will raise him up. If he has sinned, he will be forgiven."

(See also Isaiah 58:6-8; Isaiah 53:4-5; Exodus 15:26; Psalm 103:2-5; Psalm 107:20; Proverbs 3:7-8)

He has given us power over the devil, also called the thief, whose purpose here on earth is to steal, kill and destroy.

1 John 3:8
"The reason the Son of God appeared was *to destroy the devil's work.*"

Luke 10:19
"I have given you authority to trample on snakes and scorpions and to overcome *all the power of the enemy*; nothing will harm you."

1 Peter 5:8-9
"Be self-controlled and alert. Your enemy the devil prowls around like a roaring lion looking for someone to devour. *Resist him, standing firm in the faith*, because you know that your brothers throughout the world are undergoing the same kind of sufferings."

James 4:7

> "Submit yourselves, then, to God. *Resist the devil*, and he will flee from you."

(See also Ephesians 6:10-17; Colossians 2:9-10, 15; 2 Corinthians 10:4-5; 1 John 4:4; Isaiah 54:17)

God listens to and answers our prayers. He is on call 24/7.

Jeremiah 33:3

> "Call to me and *I will answer you* and tell you great and unsearchable things you do not know."

1 Peter 3:12

> "For the eyes of the Lord are on the righteous and *his ears are attentive to their prayer*, but the face of the Lord is against those who do evil."

Matthew 7:7-8

> "Ask and it will be given to you; seek and you will find; knock and the door will be opened to you. For everyone who asks receives; he who seeks finds; and to him who knocks, the door will be opened."

Philippians 4:6

> "Do not be anxious about anything, but in everything, by prayer and petition, with thanksgiving, *present your requests to God*."

Psalm 145:18

> "The Lord is near to all who call on him, to all who call on him in truth."

(See also Matthew 26:41; Ephesians 6:18; Psalm 18:6; Psalm 17:6; 1 Chronicles 5:20)

God gives wisdom to those who ask. Wisdom is considered something to be sought after, a person's supreme possession.

James 1:5
> "If any of you lacks wisdom, he should ask God, who gives generously to all without finding fault, and it will be given to him."

Proverbs 2:6
> "For the Lord gives wisdom, and from his mouth come knowledge and understanding."

Psalm 111:10
> "The fear of the Lord is the beginning of wisdom; all who follow his precepts have good understanding."

Proverbs 8:11
> "For wisdom is more precious than rubies, and nothing you desire can compare with her."

Proverbs 11:2
> "When pride comes, then comes disgrace, but with humility comes wisdom."

(See also Ephesians 1:17; Colossians 2:2-3; Proverbs 4:5-7; Proverbs 8:12-36)

He brings his peace into our minds, hearts and emotions.

John 14:27
> "Peace I leave with you; *my peace I give you.* I do not give to you as the world gives. Do not let your hearts be troubled and do not be afraid."

Philippians 4:6-7

> "Do not be anxious about anything, but in everything, by prayer and petition, with thanksgiving, present your requests to God. And the *peace of God*, which transcends all understanding, will guard your heart and your minds in Christ Jesus."

Colossians 3:15

> "*Let the peace of Christ rule* in your hearts, since as members of one body you were called to peace. And be thankful."

Psalm 29:11

> "The Lord gives strength to his people; the Lord blesses his people *with peace*."

(See also 1 Peter 3:11; 1 Corinthians 7:15, 14:33; Hebrews 12:11; 2 Thessalonians 3:16)

He provides us with spiritual gifts, which are intended to be used as we minister and encourage others. God gave the supreme gift of his Son Jesus, then sent the gift of the Holy Spirit to indwell all believers (see Acts 1:4-5). Spiritual gifts are bestowed through the work of the Holy Spirit in our lives.

1 Corinthians 12:4-6

> "There are different kinds of gifts, but the same Spirit. There are different kinds of service, but the same Lord. There are different kinds of working, but the same God works all of them in all men." Also read verses 7-11, which lists the various gifts.

Hebrews 2:4

> "God also testified to it (salvation) by signs, wonders and various miracles, and gifts of the Holy Spirit distributed according to his will."

God's Provisions – Our Heritage

Ephesians 4:7
> "Out of the generosity of Christ, each of us is given his own gift" (Message Bible).

Romans 12:6-8
> "We have different gifts, according to the grace given us. If a man's gift is prophesying, let him use it in proportion to his faith. If it is serving, let him serve; if it is teaching, let him teach; if it is encouraging, let him encourage; if it is contributing to the needs of others, let him give generously; if it is leadership, let him govern diligently; if it is showing mercy, let him do it cheerfully."

Psalm 112:9
> "He has scattered abroad his gift to the poor."

(To gain a clear understanding of these gifts, read all of 1 Corinthians chapters 12 and 14.)

<u>Jesus has prepared a place in heaven</u> so we can live with him for eternity.

John 14:2-3
> "In my Father's house are many rooms; if it were not so, I would have told you. I am going there to prepare a place for you. And if I go and prepare a place for you, I will come back and take you to be with me that you also may be where I am."

Matthew 5:11-12
> "Blessed are you when people insult you, persecute you and falsely say all kinds of evil against you because of me. Rejoice and be glad, because *great is your reward in heaven*, for in the same way they persecuted the prophets who were before you."

2 Corinthians 5:1
> "Now we know that if the earthly tent we live in is destroyed, we have a building from God, an eternal house in heaven, not built by human hands."

(See also 1 Peter 1:3-5; Matthew 6:19-21; Luke 10:20; Philippians 3:20-21)

<u>Jesus is coming again</u> for those who are expecting him.

Acts 1:11
> "Men of Galilee, they said, why do you stand here looking into the sky? This same Jesus, who has been taken from you into heaven, *will come back* in the same way you have seen him go into heaven."

1 Thess. 4:16-17
> "For the Lord himself will come down from heaven with a loud command, with the voice of the archangel and with the trumpet call of God, and the dead in Christ will rise first. After that, we who are still alive and are left will be caught up together with them in the clouds to meet the Lord in the air. And so we will be with the Lord forever."

Matthew 16:27
> "For the Son of Man is going to come in his Father's glory with his angels, and then he will reward each person according to what he has done."

(See also Mark 13:26; Revelation 1:7; 1 Thessalonians 2:19; Revelation 22:7)

God has given innumerable promises in the Bible to every believer covering almost every aspect of existence here and in eternity. They are given not only to bring us *help* but also *hope*.

That is why the promise of Jesus' coming back is important to the believer. Although the *means* for our salvation was completed when Jesus died and rose again, our full redemption is not complete until Jesus returns and we experience the resurrection of our bodies.

Hebrews 9:28
> ". . . and he will appear a second time, not to bear sin, but to bring salvation to those who are waiting for him."

Then we can claim our full inheritance as sons and daughters of our Heavenly Father. Until then, we have been given the Holy Spirit as a deposit guaranteeing that inheritance.

Ephesians 1:13-14
> "Having believed, you were marked in him with a seal, the promised Holy Spirit, who is a deposit guaranteeing our inheritance until the redemption of those who are God's possession."

Are you prepared to claim your full inheritance?

Chapter 13

GPS - to Keep Us on Track

<u>G is for Gratitude</u>

Having a grateful heart does not come naturally; it is a learned behavior which must be conscientiously cultivated. Have you ever seen a child who automatically said "thank you" without being coached over and over? In our society there is a real lack of gratitude because people "expect" certain things or feel that someone "owes" them something. It's called entitlement. This attitude certainly fosters an ungrateful spirit. Even if we don't have that attitude, we seem to find it so much easier to gripe and complain and see the negative than to look for the positive and be grateful for the daily situations that shape our lives. However, learning to be grateful and praise God is one of the most important things a Christian will ever learn. In fact, it has everything to do with faith and living in active faith has everything to do with pleasing God.

A thankful heart is one of our greatest treasures. Whenever we feel ourselves starting down that slippery slope of self-pity over an injustice or circumstance or careless word, grab onto gratitude and begin to think about all the reasons you are blessed. Name them; thank God for each blessing. It stops the spiral into sadness, despair, or even depression. Taking our thoughts captive, turning them from negative to positive, is one of those daily choices we must make.

Learn to express gratitude to others. When someone says "thank you" or shows appreciation for something we have said or done, no matter how small, it lifts our spirit. The other day after shopping at a local drug store, I took my shopping cart to where they keep the carts and meshed it with the others. Someone said, "Thank you!" Other people were around, so I looked up to see who had spoken. One of the employees was looking straight at me and again said, "Thank you for doing that." I responded, "You're welcome." He mentioned how much it helps and how few do it. I left feeling as if I had done something magnificent because one young man had a grateful heart and wasn't afraid to express it.

Thess. 5:18

> "Give thanks *in all circumstances*, for this is God's will for you in Christ Jesus."

Ephesians 5:19-20

> "Sing and make music in your heart to the Lord, always giving thanks to God the Father *for everything*, in the name of our Lord Jesus Christ."

Paul, the writer of these verses, certainly practiced what he preached! Remember the story in Acts 16 when Paul and Silas were arrested in Philippi and thrown into prison for preaching? Verse 25 says, "About midnight Paul and Silas were praying and singing hymns to God, and the other prisoners were listening to them." Notice that they weren't quiet or bashful; everyone in the jail heard them. If Paul and Silas had been like most Christians, they would have been griping and complaining instead of praying and singing. The scripture <u>might</u> have read something like this:

> About midnight Paul and Silas lay there moaning in pain. Silas whimpered, "Paul, you still there?"
> "Of course! Where else did you expect me to be?"
> "I tell you, my poor back is hurting me something awful. I don't understand why God let this happen to us. He knows we've tried to serve Him and do our best."
> "I know what you mean, Silas. If this is what we get for preaching the gospel, I think I'll quit."

Now, Paul and Silas really were in trouble . . . in a dark, filthy jail, feet in stocks, back bleeding from being beaten, in physical pain. But even though they were in jail, they didn't let the circumstances dictate their feelings. Although they were bound physically, their spirits were free. . . free to choose how they would respond to the situation. And they chose to praise God. Notice what happened as Paul and Silas praised God. Suddenly there was such a great earthquake that the foundations of the prison were shaken, all the doors were opened, and everyone's chains came loose. **Deliverance came while they were praising God!** In addition, the jailer and his whole family became believers in Jesus.

Another incident is in 2 Chronicles 20 when Jehoshaphat, the king of Israel, learned that three armies – the Ammonites, the Moabites and the inhabitants of Mount Seir – had banded together and were advancing against Israel. Jehoshaphat had no army to stand against this coming invasion, so he called a prayer meeting and the Israelites fasted and prayed. In verse 12, Jehoshaphat said to God, "We do not know what to do, but our eyes are upon you." (Great prayer!) Then God spoke through a young man in the congregation and told them not to fear or be discouraged because of this vast army. He even told them where the enemy was located. God said, "You will not have to fight this battle. The battle is not yours, but God's. Take up your positions; stand firm and see the deliverance the Lord will give you" (verse 17). Now they had to make the choice to *believe* God and *obey*, or do it their way. Verse 21 says, "After consulting the people, Jehoshaphat appointed men to sing to the Lord and to praise him for the splendor of his holiness *as they went out at the head of the army.*" In the natural, what they were doing was crazy. Instead of carrying weapons, they carried songbooks. They put the choir at the front of the whole army! Verse 22 says that "as they began to sing and praise, the Lord set ambushes against the men of Ammon and Moab and Mount Seir, and they were defeated."

Praise went *before* the deliverance. Most of the time, we wait to praise God *after* the fact, after we have received the answer. And indeed, we should remember to thank God for all the past blessings. However, we need to understand something important here. Praising God *before the fact activates our faith.* A heart full of praise is a heart that is truly trusting God. Praise is the catalyst to our faith. When you can truly praise God – before you see the answer, before anything changes, while you are still in the middle of the circumstances – you allow faith to take hold and release God's power on your behalf. I don't know how it works, I just know it does.

We need to come to the place where we are saying, "God, I praise you for who you are, King of Kings and Lord of Lords. I praise you that you hold all the power and authority and dominion. I praise you that you alone are sovereign, and I trust you to work things out in your own time and way." Someone once said, "The art of thanksgiving is thanksliving. It is gratitude in action. It is thanking God for the gift of life by living it triumphantly. It is thanking God for opportunities by accepting them as a challenge to achievement."

Psalm 34:1
> "I will bless the Lord at all times; his praise shall continually be in my mouth." (KJV)

Psalm 150:6
> "Let everything that has breath praise the Lord."

Do you have a thankful heart that expresses gratitude to God and to others?

GPS – to Keep Us on Track

<u>P is for Prayer</u>

Prayer is our hotline to God and vital to our relationship with him. Can you imagine what a relationship without communication would be? Not very healthy, to be sure. Prayer is what allows us to pour out our hearts to the One who knows us best. We can make specific requests, unload our problems, tell him our hurts and pain, and ask his help and guidance. We can express our gratitude for blessings, answered prayers, provision and protection. Most importantly, we can praise and worship him. The really cool thing about prayer is that you don't need a cell phone, land line, or satellite connection. Prayer is totally wireless with unlimited number of calls anytime day or night. You can speak aloud, whisper, or pray in complete silence. God hears you!

Jesus is our ultimate example concerning prayer. Although throngs of people would find him and follow him as he taught and healed them, Jesus often withdrew to lonely places and prayed (Luke 5:16). So must we. In the midst of our busy lives, when so many demands are made on our time and energy, we must take time to get alone with God and pray. That's where our spiritual strength and energy come from. One day when Jesus finished praying, one of his disciples asked him to teach them to pray. So he said to them, "When you pray, say: Father, hallowed be your name, your kingdom come. Give us each day our daily bread. Forgive us our sins, for we also forgive everyone who sins against us. And lead us not into temptation" (Luke 11:2-4; also see Matthew 6:9-13). Notice the order in this prayer: 1) recognize and praise God for who he is; 2) invite God's kingdom to be done on earth as it is in heaven; 3) make your requests; and 4) ask his protection from the evil one. A few verses later he adds, "So I say to you: Ask and it will be given to you; seek and you will find; knock and the door will be opened to you. For everyone who asks receives; he who seeks finds; and to him who knocks, the door will be opened" (Luke 11:9-10). Powerful prayer! Powerful promises!

Just before his arrest and ultimate death, Jesus shares many things with his disciples to give them comfort and peace, which can be found in chapters 14-17 in John's Gospel. In the three years these twelve men were with Jesus, they asked him personally many questions and received many answers. Jesus had been praying to the Father on their behalf these past three years. Now Jesus is explaining that they will soon have direct access to the Heavenly Father themselves by praying in his name. In John 16:26-27 he tells them, "In that day you will ask *in my name*. I am not saying that I will ask the Father on your behalf. No, the Father himself loves you because you have loved me and have believed that I came from God." Verse 24 says, "Until now you have not asked for anything in my name. Ask and you will receive, and your joy will be complete." This is our directive and gracious invitation to pray directly to the Father in the name of Jesus. For further study, Hebrews, chapters 9 and 10 gives a clear explanation of how the death and resurrection of Jesus changed our relationship with the Father and made Jesus our mediator.

We must also learn to listen. Jesus came to do his Father's will. He made the statement many times that he said and did only what the Father told him to say and do. His entire ministry was directed by the power of the Holy Spirit as he listened and followed his Father's instructions (see John 4:34, 8:28, 12:49-50, 14:24). In my experience, God speaks in a variety of ways as our hearts stay open to him.

One example happened early in my resolve to learn to listen. After returning home from a week teaching Vacation Bible School, I was busy in the kitchen when our five-year-old son, Todd, came to report that Shawn, who was about two years old, had put corn in his nose. One of the craft projects had been making a mosaic of dried beans and corn. I got a flashlight and looked in his nose; sure enough, there was a kernel stuck in one nostril. I got him to blow his nose as hard as possible. Nothing happened. I pressed my finger against the other nostril and had him blow again. Again nothing. I called our pediatrician and asked what I should do. He said to try again to blow it out, but not to use tweezers, as they could push the corn into his sinus cavity. If it didn't budge, I was to bring him to the office. We tried several more times to blow, but to no avail. I grabbed my purse and was herding the boys to the car when I distinctly heard, "Why don't you ask me?" I stopped dead in my tracks, then told the boys we were going to pray first. I sat Shawn on the counter top and prayed a short prayer, asking God to remove the kernel of corn from his nose. We looked at each other and waited. All of a sudden Shawn sneezed, and that corn came out of his nose and bounced across the floor. You can imagine the three of us cheering and celebrating an answer to prayer. If an all-powerful God cares enough to answer prayer for a kernel of corn in a small boy's nose, we can trust him for anything. No request is too little - or too big.

A normal day on the farm is never boring and usually presents an opportunity to either panic or pray. I have done both! A storm was coming and we needed to get our hay crop in before it rained. My husband, John, had just finished baling the coastal hay and we raced back to the field with our flat-bed truck. I drove as John loaded the bales, our two young sons bouncing along in the seat beside me. I kept watching the threatening clouds in the southwest as they grew darker and moved closer. "Lord Jesus," I prayed, "please help us get this hay in without getting it wet." Wet baled hay is almost impossible to dry out and often molds. "Lord, we really need this hay crop. Please slow the storm."

Just then I saw another truck pull into the field. "Thank you, Lord, for extra help." Alert to our dilemma, our neighbor and his two sons had come to help and quickly began loading hay. Even as fast as we worked, the storm seemed to be coming faster. The wind began to blow harder, swirling particles of hay across the field in a frenzied dance. The fragrance of freshly cut hay now mingled with the smell of rain. As I guided the truck between the rows of hay, I kept glancing in the direction of the approaching storm. Only a few minutes and we would need to head for the barn. Hundreds of bales still lay in the field. "Oh, Lord, please help us." Now I could clearly see a wall of water moving toward us about a half mile away. I watched as the heavy gray sheet inched its way across the fields, drenching everything in its path and obliterating the landscape behind it. Desperately I cried out, "Father, I ask you in the name of Jesus to turn that storm and cause it to go around us." I held my breath as large drops of water splattered on the windshield. Then, in amazement, I watched as that gray wall of water came up to the road that borders our property on the south, a thousand feet or so from the field, and simply moved east. Those few drops were all the rain that fell on our hay. Not only can God calm a storm, he can change the direction of one, too.

"Call to me and I will answer you and tell you great and unsearchable things you do not know" (Jeremiah 33:3). Yes, he does! "The Lord will guide you always" (Isaiah 58:11). And he will!

> *Are you experiencing the power of prayer?*

P is also for People

You are now a member of God's family and in a covenant relationship with other believers. It's important to find a Bible-believing church that fosters spiritual growth. The loving fellowship and encouragement from a good church family will help to strengthen your faith, aid you on your journey, and provide accountability.

Acts 2:42
> The first believers "devoted themselves to the apostles' teaching, to fellowship, to breaking of bread, and to prayer."

1 Thess. 5:11
> "Therefore encourage one another and build each other up, just as in fact you are doing."

(See also 1 John 1:7; Ephesians 2:19; Romans 8:15)

Is attending church criteria for maintaining our salvation? No, it's not. However, Hebrews 10:25 admonishes us to "not give up meeting together, as some are in the habit of doing." Why? Because we need each other; we need more mature believers to walk with us. As we have already discussed, salvation is both an event and a process. Left without encouragement and nourishment, it's easy for a new Christian, or any Christian for that matter, to slip back into their "old nature" ways of thinking and behaving. We were created for fellowship and we can find tremendous encouragement from other believers as we worship, pray, and study together. Some people are not physically able to attend church services, some live in remote areas with limited access to a church, others work when most churches hold services. In these cases, other options can be pursued, such as Christian radio and television broadcasts or CD's and DVD's. Others feel more comfortable in a small study or fellowship group, which is a great way to get to know others who have embarked on the same journey as you. Maintaining interaction and sharing with one another can create strong relationships which will prove vital in helping you mature as a Christian. No matter your circumstances, find a way to incorporate and maintain fellowship with other believers.

> *Are you seeking fellowship with other believers?*

If you are looking for a perfect church with perfect people, you will be disappointed. There is no such thing! All of us are imperfect, every one of us have flaws; we are each "in process." Most of those who refuse to attend church have met with some degree of disillusionment by words or actions of those who are in the church. Hypocrisy is high on the list of "sins" we hate. Jesus hated hypocrisy, too. He called out the teachers of the law and Pharisees time and again for teaching one thing and practicing something else (see Matthew 23:1-36 for an example). The bottom line of hypocrisy is dishonesty: appearing to be something we are not, putting on the act of respectability when our hearts are far from God, or teaching and preaching things we are not willing to practice ourselves. Many people use this as an excuse to not attend church. However, if each of us were willing to take an honest look at ourselves, we would likely find areas of dishonesty and hypocrisy. Remember the speck and the plank comparison about taking the plank out of our own eye so we can see clearly to remove the speck in our neighbor's eye? (Matthew 7:1-5) That's what it's all about – judging ourselves first. In John 8, when the religious leaders brought to Jesus a woman who had been caught in adultery, they reminded him that the Law of Moses commanded stoning such a woman. "Now what do you say?" they asked. Of course, they were trying to trap Jesus, but he answered, "If any one of you is without sin, let him be the first to throw a stone at her." One by one her accusers began to back away and leave until only the woman and Jesus were left. "Woman, where are they? Has no one condemned you?" "No one, sir," she said. "Then neither do I condemn you. Go now and leave your life of sin." The sins of her accusers disqualified them from judging her. So do ours.

Jesus had just told the crowd that unless their righteousness surpassed that of the Pharisees and teachers of the law (the hypocrites), they would certainly not enter the kingdom of heaven. Then he said, "You have heard that it was said to the people long ago, 'Do not murder' and anyone who murders will be subject to judgment. But I tell you that anyone who is angry with his brother will be subject to judgment. Again, anyone who says to his brother, 'Raca,' is answerable to the Sanhedrin. But anyone who says, 'You fool!' will be in danger of the fire of hell" (Matthew 5:21-22). Jesus is talking about heart issues that indicate who we really are. What we harbor in our hearts will come out of our mouths and can eventually determine our actions.

Luke 6:45

> "The good man brings good things out of the good stored up in his heart, and the evil man brings evil things out of the evil stored up in his heart. For out of the overflow of his heart his mouth speaks."

How many times have we made contemptuous remarks about others? How many acts of violence are the fruit of anger? We are grieving the Holy Spirit if we allow unwholesome talk to come out of our mouths or harbor "bitterness, rage and anger, brawling and slander, along with every form of malice" (Ephesians 4:29-31). Why? Left unchecked, these things will wreck our lives. We are told to get rid of them. Plus, we are violating one of the most important commandments – *to love*. "If anyone says, 'I love God,' yet hates his brother, he is a liar. For anyone who does not love his brother, whom he has seen, cannot love God, whom he has not seen. And he has given us this command: whoever loves God must also love his brother" (1 John 4:20-21).We are lying with our lives, we are hypocrites, if we say we love God but don't love others.

> *Are you open and honest by the way you live?*

S is for Study

There is **no** substitute for personal reading and studying the Scriptures. Tons of great inspirational books and study materials are also available to teach and encourage, which can be of tremendous value for your spiritual growth. However, the Bible is literally *God's words to us*. While Jesus is the Living Word, the Bible is God's written Word and contains his covenant and his promises to us.

2 Timothy 3:15
> ". . . the holy Scriptures... are able to make you wise for salvation through faith in Christ Jesus."

2 Timothy 3:16, 17
> "All scripture is *God-breathed* and is useful for teaching, rebuking, correcting and training in righteousness, so that the man of God may be thoroughly equipped for every good work."

(See also 2 Peter 1:21; Matthew 4:4; Isaiah 55:10a, 11; Jeremiah 1:12; Psalm 138:2b; Psalm 119:89; Matthew 24:35; John 6:68)

The one unfolding story throughout the Bible is God's redemption of man. We, the crowning achievement of all his creation, are so important to God that he wrote an entire book for us. God wants us to know how to live on planet earth, as well as how to live eternally. The Message Bible says it well:

Hebrews 4:12-13

> "God means what he says. What he says goes. His powerful Word is sharp as a surgeon's scalpel, cutting through everything, whether doubt or defense, laying us open to listen and obey. Nothing and no one is impervious to God's Word. We can't get away from it – no matter what."

When we begin to *believe* the Word of God above what we see or feel or even understand in our present circumstances, then we begin to tap into the vast resources God has provided for us. We move beyond our own cleverness or ability to figure things out and begin to rely on God and his faithfulness to fulfill his Word in our lives. <u>And that's what faith is</u>: *it's believing and accepting that what God said is true.*

A great benefit is reading the Bible <u>aloud</u>. Romans 10:17 tells us that "faith comes from hearing the message" or the Word of God. As you literally "hear" the Word of God spoken out of your own mouth, *faith* will begin to grow inside you. It's not faith in your own abilities, your job, the medical profession, your bank account, other people, or even your prayers. It is faith in God and *his* ability, *his* unlimited resources, and *his* desire to provide for all our needs "so that you may be filled to the measure of all the fullness of God" (Ephesians 3:19). As the Scriptures become indelibly etched in your mind and heart, you will understand the difference in having faith in God versus having faith in someone or something else.

Matthew 17:20

> ". . . I tell you the truth, if you have faith as small as a mustard seed, you can say to this mountain, move from here to there and it will move. Nothing will be impossible for you."

On a number of occasions, Jesus told his disciples they had "little faith" (Matthew 8:26, 14:31, 16:8). He also marveled at "great faith" as displayed in the centurion, who came to Jesus because his servant was about to die (Luke 7:9). Another time, when Jesus visited his hometown, he was not able to do many miracles because of their "lack of faith" (Mark 6:1-6). Little faith, great faith, and no faith. In each instance, those he spoke to either knew about him, knew his family, or had traveled with him. What made the difference in the measure of faith they exhibited was what they chose to believe about who he was. Those of "little faith" were awed at what he did, but had not yet come to acknowledge him as the Divine Son of God. Those who expressed great faith had heard or seen the miracles and believed in him and his ability to do the supernatural, whether heal, feed the multitudes, or raise the dead. Many of the people in Jesus' hometown were amazed at his wisdom and miracles, but discounted his authenticity and were offended, since they *knew* he was the carpenter's son. They saw no reason to believe he was different from any of them.

Without exception, our faith is what we do with the understanding we have about who Jesus is. Do we understand and believe he's the Son of God who died to pay for our sins? Do we believe he was resurrected, thus conquering death, hell, and the grave? Do we believe salvation can be found in no other person except Jesus? Do we accept that nothing is impossible to those who believe? That's what God told us in his Word. We have a choice to make. It's that simple! Mark chapter 9 relates the story of the father who brought to Jesus his son, who was possessed by a deaf and mute spirit that threw him into convulsions. Jesus asked the boy's father, "How long has he been like this?" "From childhood," the father answered. "It has often thrown him into fire or water to kill him, but if you can do anything, take pity on us and help us." Jesus told him, "Everything is possible for him who believes." Immediately the boy's father exclaimed, "I do believe; help me overcome my unbelief!" This can be our cry, too – I do believe! Help my unbelief!

> *Is your faith little or large?*
> *Is it growing?*

GPS – to Keep Us on Track

Chapter 14

Wrapping It Up

Have you ever thought of living forever and ever and ever and ever, on and on with no end? My mind tries to grasp it, but I cannot. The life I live now has a beginning and a seeming end – birth, death, and in between. That I can grasp. But eternity? Living forever after this life is spent? That's too much for my finite mind to comprehend. To think that the same God who created the universe with all its planets and galaxies, the same God who planned, designed, and brought into being every living creature and everything to sustain life, has also made preparation for all mankind to live with him forever. That thought is far too wonderful for me to understand. But He has done just that! And that, my friend, is what life is all about – preparing mankind, making us ready to live forever with an absolutely holy and just, all powerful, all knowing God. Hebrews 12:14 tells us, "Make every effort to live in peace with all men and *to be holy*; without holiness no one will see the Lord." First Peter 1:13-16 tells us, "Therefore, prepare your minds for action; be self-controlled; set your hope fully on the grace to be given you when Jesus Christ is revealed. As obedient children, do not conform to the evil desires you had when you lived in ignorance. But just as he who called you is holy, so *be holy in all you do*; for it is written: 'Be holy, because I am holy.'"

So what is holiness? I'm not a saint and I certainly don't feel holy. So does God expect me to be perfect? Although perfection and holiness are often used interchangeably, they are not the same. Perfection speaks of total sinlessness, which none of us will achieve on our own this side of heaven. Only Jesus was totally sinless, and we are made perfect in God's sight through Jesus' death and resurrection. Holiness means "set apart" for God,

Wrapping It Up

"set apart" from sinful living. We are now being made holy by the work of the Holy Spirit as we live our lives, making the daily choices to honor God in all we think, say, and do. Hebrews 10:14 says it all: "By one sacrifice he (Jesus) *has made perfect forever those who are being made holy.*" It's not about trying hard enough, it's all about letting God be God in your life. You are being made holy as you submit to the work of the Holy Spirit in you.

> *Are the words of my mouth*
> *and the meditation of my heart*
> *pleasing in your sight, Lord?*
> *(Psalm 19:14)*

The question, "Am I really a Christian?" can only be answered by you, dear friend. Only you can make the decision to be a Christ follower. You are the only one responsible for making the daily choices to walk in obedience to truth as set forth in God's Word. No one can do that for you – not your church, pastor, priest, parents, spouse, or friends. They can certainly walk beside you, encourage and help you understand and grow, but they are not ultimately responsible for where you spend eternity. <u>*But you are never alone!*</u> God has given you the Holy Spirit to dwell in you. Your body is the "temple" or living quarters of the Holy Spirit. He will be your constant companion to teach, help, empower, correct, convict, guide and comfort. He also intercedes for you in accordance with God's will, produces good fruit in your attitudes and actions, and develops spiritual gifts in you. *What an awesome companion!*

Second Peter 3:9 tells us plainly that God is patient with us, not wanting anyone to perish, but desiring everyone to come to repentance. If you have never experienced the love of God in your life and do not have the assurance of salvation, or if you want to renew your commitment to Him, open your heart to the Holy Spirit now. He desires to fill your heart with His presence and bring all the blessings of His love into your life.

Speaking the Truth

After you have become a Christ follower, learning and understanding the truth about who you are and what God has promised you as his child will keep you anchored. When Satan comes with his lies and deception, *applying the truth wins every time*. However, if you do not know the truth, you cannot apply it. The following are statements of truth straight from the One who created you and wrote the Book for you. You are encouraged to read or speak these aloud daily until they become firmly established in your mind and heart. These statements are only a tiny drop in the vast ocean of wisdom and truth found in God's Word. You will keep discovering more and more as you read and study the Bible.

Who I am:

- I am loved. *1 John 3:1 & 4:19, Romans 8:35-39*
- I am forgiven. *1 John 1:9, Psalm 130:3-4*
- I am justified, declared "not guilty" by a just God. *Romans 4:25; 5:1 & 9*
- I am purified from all sin and unrighteousness. *1 John 1:7 & 9*
- I am a child of God, adopted into his family. *Romans 8:16, Ephesians 1:5*
- I am a new creation; the old has gone, the new has come. *2 Corinthians 5:17, Ephesians 4:22-23*
- I am an heir of God and a joint heir with Christ Jesus. *Galatians 4:6-7, Romans 8:17*

Wrapping It Up

- I am free from the power of sin. *Romans 6:18 & 8:2*
- I am strong in the Lord and his mighty power. *Ephesians 6:10*
- I am more than a conqueror. *Romans 8:37, 1 Corinthians 15:57, 1 John 4:4*
- I am an overcomer. *1 John 5:4-5, Romans 12:21, Rev. 12:11*
- I am the righteousness of God in Christ Jesus. *2 Corinthians 5:21*
- I am God's fellow worker. *1 Corinthians 3:9*
- I am seated in the heavenly realms in Christ Jesus. *Ephesians 2:6-7*

What I've been given:

- I have been rescued from the kingdom of darkness and brought into the kingdom of light. *Colossians 1:13-14*
- I have the assurance of eternal life. *1 John 5:11-13, John 17:1-3*
- I have Christ, who now dwells in my heart through faith. *Ephesians 3:17*
- I have the Holy Spirit living in me. *1 Corinthians 3:16, Ephesians 2:22*
- I have the mind of Christ. *1 Corinthians 2:16*
- I have been given spiritual gifts to use to encourage and benefit others. *1 Corinthians 12:4, 7-11*
- Nothing can separate me from God's love. *Romans 8:35-39*
- God is with me forever. *Hebrews 13:5, Matthew 28:20, Psalm 27:10*
- I have God's guidance. *Isaiah 48:17 & 58:11, Proverbs 3:6*
- Since God is for me, no one can stand against me. *Romans 8:31*
- I have authority over all the power of the enemy; nothing will harm me. *Luke 10:19*

Wrapping It Up

- I have been given ways and means with which to fight the evil one. *Ephesians 6:10-12 & 13-17, Isaiah 54:17, 2 Corinthians 10:4-5, James 4:7, 1 Peter 5:8-9, 1 John 4:3-4*
- God makes me stand firm in Christ. *2 Corinthians 1:21*
- I have God's protection and help in trouble. *Psalm 91, Proverbs 12:21, Psalm 37:28, 2 Timothy 4:18, Psalm 46:1-2*
- I have peace that transcends all understanding. *Philippians 4:7, John 14:27*
- I have the comfort of God in all my troubles and he rescues me. *2 Corinthians 1:3-4, Isaiah 61:1-3, Psalm 34:19 & 50:15*
- I have been provided healing and health. *1 Peter 2:24, James 5:14-15, Psalm 103:2-3, Isaiah 53:5 & 58:7-8*
- I have all my needs met. *Philippians 4:19, Psalm 23:1*
- I have the joy of the Lord. *Nehemiah 8:10*
- God gives me strength. *Colossians 1:11, Isaiah 40:29-31, Philippians 4:13, Psalm 28:7*
- I have been blessed with every spiritual blessing in Christ Jesus. *Ephesians 1:3*
- I will receive the crown of life. *James 1:12, 1 Corinthians 9:24-25*

<u>How I intend to live:</u>

- I will grow in the knowledge of God. *Colossians 1:10, 2 Peter 1:5-8 & 3:17-18*
- I will live by faith in Christ Jesus, not by sight, because without faith it is impossible to please God. *Galatians 2:20, 2 Corinthians 5:7, Romans 1:17, Hebrews 11:6, Philippians 3:9*
- I will love the Lord with all my heart, soul, mind and strength. *Mark 12:30*
- I will forgive others as the Lord has forgiven me. *Colossians 3:13, Matthew 18:21-22*
- I will be quick to listen, slow to speak, and slow to become angry. *James 1:19*

Wrapping It Up

- I will exercise self-control.
  Proverbs 29:11, Galatians 5:22-23
- As much as it is in my power, I will live at peace with everyone. *Hebrews 12:14*
- I will work at whatever I do with all my heart, as working for the Lord. *Colossians 3:23*
- I can do everything through him who gives me strength. *Philippians 4:13*
- Sin will not control my thoughts, attitudes or actions. *Romans 6:11-14, 2 Corinthians 10:5, Ephesians 4:31*
- I will keep a tight rein on my tongue, so that my mouth will not sin.
  Psalm 17:3, James 1:26, Ephesians 4:29
- I will seek to have an undivided heart that fears God's name. *Psalm 86:11, Jeremiah 24:7*
- I will reject the wrong and choose the right.
  2 Thessalonians 3:13, Romans 12:17
- I will walk in love toward others.
  2 John 6, Romans 13:8, Matthew 5:43-44, 1 John 3:18, Proverbs 10:12, Ephesians 4:2
- I will walk in obedience to God's commands.
  2 John 6, John 14:15, 15:10, 1 John 2:3-5
- I will not be overcome by evil, but will overcome evil with good. *Romans 12:21*
- I will persevere and not give up.
  Hebrews 10:36, James 1:4
- I will abound in every good work. *2 Corinthians 9:8, Ephesians 2:10, 2 Timothy 2:21, Colossians 1:10*
- I will not live in fear, timidity or anxiety, but will allow God to handle my cares. *1 Peter 5:7, Philippians 4:6, 2 Timothy 1:7, Psalm 23:4, 34:4, 55:22 & 94:19, Isaiah 35:3-4 & 41:10, Psalm 112:7*
- I will fight the good fight of faith and take hold of eternal life. *1 Timothy 6:12, Romans 6:22*
- I will not be foolish, but understand what the Lord's will is. *Ephesians 5:17, Isaiah 48:17, Psalm 31:3 & 32:8, Proverbs 16:9 & 19:21, Jeremiah 29:11*

Wrapping It Up

- I will allow the Holy Spirit to search my heart and reveal anything offensive. *Psalm 139:23-24*
- I will set a godly example for others to follow. *1 Timothy 4:12, Titus 2:7*

In Summary:

1. Believe and receive *everything* God has for you according to His plan
2. Embrace grace; live in truth
3. Gaze at God; glimpse at self
4. Cultivate gratitude and a positive attitude
5. Overcome instead of being overrun
6. Walk in love and forgiveness
7. Hold on; continue; persevere to the end
8. Then we can say with the Apostle Paul, "I have fought the good fight, I have finished the race, I have kept the faith. Now there is in store for me the crown of righteousness, which the Lord, the righteous Judge, will award to me on that day – and not only to me, but also to all who have longed for his appearing." (2 Timothy 4:7-8).

> *"I write these things to you who believe in the name of the Son of God so that you may know that you have eternal life."*
> *1 John 5:13*

Wrapping It Up

HELPFUL RESOURCES

Barker, Kenneth, General Editor. *The NIV Study Bible.* Grand Rapids, MI: Zondervan Bible Publishers, 1985.

Goodrick, Edward W. And John R. Kohlenberger III. *The NIV Exhaustive Concordance.* Grand Rapids, MI: Zondervan Publishing House, 1990.

Gothard, Bill, Founder. *Institute in Basic Life Principles.* Oak Brook, IL: Advanced Training Institute International, 1996.

Gray, James M., D.D. *The Concise Bible Commentary.* Peabody, MA: Hendrickson Publishers, Inc., 1999.

Guralnik, David B., Editor in Chief. *Webster's New World Dictionary.* Cleveland, OH: Simon and Schuster, 1984.

Kennedy, D. James. *Truths That Transform.* Grand Rapids, MI: Fleming H. Revell, 1996.

Life Application Bible, New International Version. Wheaton, IL: Tyndale House Publishers, Inc. and Grand Rapids, MI: Zondervan Publishing House, 1991.

Little, Paul. *Know Why You Believe.* Downers Grove, IL: InterVarsity Press, 1988.

McDowell, Josh and Don Stewart. *Answers to Tough Questions.* San Bernardino, CA: Here's Life Publishers, Inc., 1980.

McDowell, Josh and Don Stewart. *Reasons Skeptics Should Consider Christianity*. San Bernardino, CA: Here's Life Publishers, Inc., 1981.

McDowell, Josh. *The New Evidence That Demands a Verdict*. Nashville, TN: Thomas Nelson Publishers, 1999.

Morris, Henry M. Ph.D. *Many Infallible Proofs*. El Cajon, CA: Creation Life Publisher, Inc., 1974.

Peterson, Eugene H. *The Message Bible*. Colorado Springs, CO: Navpress, 2002.

Pettingill, William L. and R. A. Torrey. *1001 Bible Questions Answered*. New York, NY: Inspirational Press, 1997.

Phillips, Bob. *Covenant: Its Blessings – Its Curses*. Lindale, TX: World Challenge, Inc., 1986.

Three-In-One Concise Bible Reference Companion. Nashville, TN: Thomas Nelson Publishers, 1982.

Am I Really a Christian?

Am I Really a Christian?

ABOUT THE AUTHOR

Dorothy Smith was born in Bowling Green, Ohio, but moved to Texas with her family when she was in junior high school. Her father was a pastor, so she literally grew up in church. She credits her parents for instilling in her a love for studying and teaching God's Word, as well as encouraging her to memorize Scripture.

Little did this city girl from Ohio know she would one day become a farmer's wife and learn to drive trucks and tractors, herd cattle and help meet the demands of farm life. Would she trade for any other lifestyle? Never! They still live on the farm where her husband, John, was born and still raise cattle and crops. Their two sons started driving and operating equipment at a very young age, taking over various aspects of the farm work as they became old enough. The Lord has blessed them with six precious grandchildren.

Through the years, God put many challenges before them. One challenge was getting an obscenity ordinance passed in their city, which successfully closed down a drive-in theater showing x-rated movies on a bigger-than-life screen and removed books and magazines with offensive covers out of public view. Another challenge was opening their home to many teenagers and young adults, who needed extra love and support or a place to stay for a season. Facing situations bigger than they knew how to handle, prayer became an integral part of life and still is. Dorothy established and led the prayer ministry in their church for many years, and then stepped outside the walls of the church to coordinate the National Day of Prayer in Denton. She also helped organize the Denton County Christian Prayer Gatherings, which crosses denominational and ethnic lines and meets monthly to pray over issues in their communities, state and nation.

For pleasure and relaxation, Dorothy loves playing the piano. She began showing an interest at age five, when she would play by ear the songs her sister was practicing. Largely self-taught, she started playing for church as a teenager and remained active in the music ministry for many years.

Through the years she has worn many hats, including owning and operating her own resume writing business and working in office management and bookkeeping positions. Dorothy currently volunteers for a Pro-life Pregnancy Resource Center in their resale store and recently became an advocate in the clinic, which provides opportunities for one-on-one ministry to young women. She and her husband attend Cross Timbers Community Church in Argyle, Texas.

Am I Really a Christian?

Am I Really a Christian?

Am I Really a Christian?

Am I Really a Christian?

www.ingramcontent.com/pod-product-compliance
Lightning Source LLC
Chambersburg PA
CBHW021125300426
44113CB00006B/302